UBUNTU

UBUNTU

THE SPIRIT OF AFRICAN
TRANSFORMATION MANAGEMENT

Lovemore Mbigi with Jenny Maree

1995
KNOWLEDGE RESOURCES (PTY) LTD

ISBN 1-874997-04-7

First Edition, second impression 1995.
Published in 1995 by
Knowledge Resources (Pty) Ltd
P O Box 3954
RANDBURG, 2125
Tel: (011) 880-8540
Fax: (011) 880-8700

Printed and bound by Sigma Press, Pretoria
Cover design by Pentagraph (Pty) Ltd, Johannesburg

FOREWORD/
ACKNOWLEDGEMENTS

This book is not an academic treatise, but rather anecdotes and observations personally experienced by two simple Africans who are interested in transforming South African organisations. The style has been deliberately borrowed from African traditional story telling and you may find it highflown, fastmoving and simplistic.

We would like to thank Neil Cumming for being a mentor to both of us and showing great tolerance for innovative thinking.

Our gratitude also goes to the spirit of Dembetembe for having given one of the authors his early education and the spiritual roots of which he is proud.

Gratitude also goes to Ronnie Lessem for continued intellectual support and inspiration.

CONTENTS

INTRODUCTION
THE RELEVANCE OF UBUNTU IN AFRICAN MANAGEMENT

The deep running water
Is a fortress filled
With lores and mysteries of amaXhosa
Its depths hide answers
To numerous questions
Its powers hypnotise and transform
The chosen succumb to the calling
And join the people from the other world

The Other World by Mzi Mahola
From the Anthology *Strange Things*

Ubuntu is a metaphor that describes the significance of group solidarity, on survival issues, that is so central to the survival of African communities, who as a result of the poverty and deprivation have to survive through brotherly group care and not individual self-reliance. This practice of collective unity is not new and not peculiar to Africa. All dispossessed groups wherever they are in the world, Harlem in New York, Brixton in the UK, subscribe in practice to this concept of Ubuntu. It is a concept of brotherhood and collective unity for survival among the poor in every society. It can also be called "Umfowethu" in Zulu or a son of the soil, and in Shona it is "Mwana wevhu" or "pachedu".

In essence Ubuntu is a universal concept that can be applicable to all poor communities. It is of relevance to approaches of urban renewal in the ghetto or inner cities of the West as well as community development in rural and peri-urban situations in developing countries. It is also universal in that it can be

1

applied to the challenge of empowering marginalised minorities in the West and shop-floor employees anywhere in the world.

The cardinal belief of Ubuntu is that *a man can only be a man through others*. In its most fundamental sense it stands for *personhood* and *morality*. In the Shona tribe this would be called Unhu or Ubuntu (hereafter referred to only as Ubuntu).

The key values of Ubuntu are as follows:

GROUP SOLIDARITY, CONFORMITY, COMPASSION, RESPECT, HUMAN DIGNITY AND COLLECTIVE UNITY

It is our belief that unless the development structures, strategies and processes can harness these Ubuntu values into a dynamic transformative force for reconstruction and development, failure will be almost certain.

For African organisations and companies the challenges of social and political innovation far exceed the technical challenges. Our suggestion is that we must harness the social experience and innovation of the African people and align them with successful management techniques from the West and the East. In essence this requires careful and creative strategic alignment by African managers. It can not be imported from either Japan or the West. This has to be done locally by managers and intellectuals who understand our own situational reality and survival agenda. It requires us to draw on the strength of our own cultural diversity and our triple heritage from Africa, the East and the West.

The most pervasive and fundamental collective experience of the African people is their religious experience. It is integrated into all aspects of their lives on a daily basis. It is therefore important that conceptual frameworks of powerful strategic ideas must try and make reference to the African religious and cultural experience if effective transfer and adaptation are to take place. Preferably the significant ideas and practices must be translated from the foreign languages into the relevant local language.

It is in this respect that the following four theories and the concept of Ubuntu in this book will be a humble beginning in this direction:-

- **The concept of Ubuntu, which is the *collective solidarity* of the poor on survival issues.**

- **The *Corpse Shadow Theory*, which focuses on the need to burn the past before renewal and a new vision can occur.**

- **The *Nhorowondo Theory*, which emphasises the need to appreciate the historical roots of any technique in order to adapt it successfully.**

- **The *Collective Fingers Theory*, which tries to emphasise the importance of collective education and rituals in order to manage change in Africa successfully.**

- **The *Rainbow African Spirits Theory*, (Dembetembe) which symbolically and metaphorically represents possible dominant cultural elements or dimensions in organisations.**

The concept of Ubuntu emphasises the need to harness the solidarity tendency of the African people in developing management practices and approaches. It is important for us to adopt some Western and Eastern management techniques, but

3

these will only enable African organisations to attain competitive parity.

Imitations will not give us competitive advantage. We need to attain **competitive space** and **competitive advantage** through creating and doing something that has never been done before, with customers, in terms of production and management practices. The management practices need to be uniquely African in orientation.

The only way poor organisations and poor societies can create competitive space for themselves is through transformative processes and practices. The union movement in its fight against Apartheid has demonstrated that the collective solidarity of the African people can be harnessed for transformative purposes. The union was always "caucusing" and going back to its constituency to get the mandate on key issues during discussions and negotiations with management.

It also unleashed the energy and the collective solidarity of its members through collective rituals and mass rallies; speeches were punctuated with traditional songs and dancing just as in the traditional public meetings and ceremonies.

If collective solidarity practices could be used by unions to democratise South African society and companies, it could also be used to create competitive space and advantage in the new South Africa.

Africa's achievements and genius do not lie in technology but in **social** and **spiritual** spheres. If Africa is going to enter and win in the global economic arena, it will have to draw on its spiritual and social heritage. The beautiful things in Africa still have to be created. Social innovation, of which the crafting of relevant organisational collective rituals and ceremonies is an important dimension, has to be brought to the centre of organisational transformation and renewal in Africa.

Fortunately, for us in Africa, in the global competitive game there are not permanent winners and losers. Africa's day is about to come. Despite pessimism the sun will soon shine on the beautiful face of Africa. We must not despair! The great rich countries of today were once poor nations. Our intention to sail beyond sunset must remain unshakable.

For this to happen, Africa needs to accelerate its learning curve by articulating what it is going through and reflecting on the experience. In Africa we must realise that the traditional African society had its own institutions which functioned well on certain well-tried principles and practices.

It is important to build on these indigenous cultural practices if the need for rapid assimilation of foreign Western and Eastern practices is going to be met rapidly and successfully. Ali Mazrui, a Kenyan and American based intellectual, in a BBC documentary entitled "The Africans" said, *"But in the final analysis the shallowness of the imported institutions is due to that culture gap between the new structures and ancient values, between alien institutions and ancestral traditions. Africa can never go back completely to its pre-colonial starting point but there may be a case for at least a partial retreat, a case for re-establishing contacts with familiar landmarks of yesteryear and restarting the journey of modernisation under indigenous impetus"*.

The assimilation of Western culture has not been very successful. Africa needs to draw on its triple cultural heritage from Africa, the East and the West. The starting point should be our own roots if we are to meet the challenges of development and reconstruction. As Amilcar Cabral, the leader of PAIGG, the nationalist resistance movement in Guinea-

Bissau, says, *"A people who free themselves from foreign domination will not be culturally free unless, without underestimating the importance of positive contributions from the oppressor's culture and the other cultures, they return to the upwards paths of their own culture"*. (Translated from the Portuguese.)

It is possible that the Afrikaners are the only people who have genuinely tried to develop a written African language and to domesticate Western culture and technology through their own collective cultural experience, creatively. Just as black Africans still have to rise to this challenge, so do the white Africans with English, Dutch, German and French roots. The Asian tigers success stories seem to suggest that effective adoption of foreign business and management practices and technologies requires an indigenous cultural renaissance. The writing of ideas in the vernacular languages is a crucial element of this renaissance. There is no recorded case in human history where people undertook a revolution in business and development without a cultural revolution.

Our view is that if Africans are going to undertake the challenge of development they need to discover their own collective self-identity. This has to be an inward journey which should lead to a celebration of collective "personhood" which we have called Ubuntu.

CHAPTER 1

THE SPIRIT OF UBUNTU IN AFRICAN MANAGEMENT

It is the call
Of a timeless glory
And the beat of the native song
That beckoned you to struggle on

The white night is dead
Freedom walks in the sunrise
And in the glow
Of an eternal love song

From the poem **Zimbabwean Love Song**
by Don Mattera
From the Anthology *Azanian Love Songs*

THE ROOTS OF UBUNTU

Disadvantaged or marginalised groups anywhere in the world survive on collective unity or solidarity and consciousness. Due to the poverty of their material circumstances, they cannot survive on individual initiative only. They have to stick together on selective survival issues and unquestioning conformity is expected from everyone on these issues. Loyalty and conformity become prized values for every member of the group. The ability to sacrifice, suffer and display a spirit of service with regard to certain selected survival issues, becomes a mark of heroism. The failure to conform on survival issues such as rent boycotts, mass action, strikes and liberation is met with ruthless measures.

Therefore the spirit of patriotism is an important part of Ubuntu. This preparedness to die for one's group is what drives activists and nationalist movements. The spirit was a transformative force in the union movement and the mass democratic movement in this country. South Africa owes the birth of its nation to the emancipating spirit of Ubuntu. It drives the national change process towards national liberation and majority rule, but not sufficiently to meet the challenges of reconstruction and development.

UBUNTU AS A SOCIAL SURVIVAL STRATEGY

The challenge then is to build into the spirit of Ubuntu, a new dimension of citizenship. This is the ability to live for one's country; the ability to take personal accountability and responsibility for improving one's situation. This is perhaps the missing link and dimension of Ubuntu in post-independent Africa. If the solidarity principle of Ubuntu is to survive beyond the fight for liberation, it has to become dynamic and undergo transformation to add the important dimension of citizenship and personal stewardship.

In South African companies, the solidarity principle was the most dynamic and transformational force as manifested by the shop steward movement.

It is important not to marginalise this solidarity spirit of Ubuntu in the new South Africa. Our opinion is that we must try to build on the collective spirit of Ubuntu and harness it for productivity and competitive purposes. At a national level we need to harness it in order to manage the challenges of reconstruction and development. We need a new inclusive national vision.

Ubuntu can serve as a starting point for building this collective national vision. Ubuntu can help organisations to develop corporate citizenship. By building the solidarity spirit of Ubuntu it is possible to build co-operation and competitive strategies by allowing teamwork to permeate the whole organisation. It will also help us to find a new identity as a nation; a new identity which will transcend the ethnic divisions that haunt us. It is in the spirit of Ubuntu, with its emphasis on working together and respecting human dignity, that we can find our way forward.

The spirit of Ubuntu may help define a new critical path towards the new South Africa. If companies are going to be competitive, they will need to develop a tradition of working together on survival and competitive issues. The collective experience of the black people in South Africa can help us to do this and we need to build on it.

The proposal being made is that we need an innovative way to manage in the new South Africa based on our collective experience and the lessons we have learnt so far in the struggle. The new way must be a package of solutions that would address the survival challenges of global competition, as well as reconstruction and development.

The approach would also need to incorporate the global experience of other developing countries such as Latin America and Asia. The constant reliance on Europe and the West as the only model for managerial practice and development may be too limited. The authors are not saying neglect the Western experience, but that our starting point is to harness the South African collective cultural experience and then synthesise it with recent experiences from other developing countries - Asia and Latin America. **We call for a celebration of global citizenship where we can be both tribal and cosmopolitan**.

9

We therefore argue for the need to come up with a developmental approach to management in South Africa. It will not be possible for South African managers to ignore the reality of underdevelopment in their societies. It is our opinion that this approach should be based on collective solidarity and teamwork, but focusing on developmental challenges which could be the survival answer for South African organisations.

The development approach has to focus on the reframing of people's minds and issues relevant to restructuring of societies and institutions - renewing the spirit and morale of the people and the re-engineering of processes and practices. This can help companies and institutions to be competitive and to engage in the solving of thorny problems of development and corporate renewal.

UBUNTU MANAGEMENT APPROACH

The Ubuntu management approach must have the following outcomes:-

- The development of co-operative and competitive **PEOPLE**

- The development of co-operative and competitive **PARADIGMS** and **PERSPECTIVES**

- The development of co-operative and competitive **PRACTICES**

- The development of co-operative and competitive **PROCESSES**

- The development of co-operative and competitive **POLICIES** and **PROCEDURES**

- Finally, the development of co-operative and competitive **VALUES** as well as **INSTITUTIONS**

10

DEVELOPMENT OF CO-OPERATIVE
AND COMPETITIVE PEOPLE

One of the major reasons why South Africa is not competitive is that the majority of its people have not been developed in terms of skills and knowledge. South Africa's competitive ranking ever since 1992 has been very low on this dimension. Education has been neglected for a long time and the government in 1953 under the inspiration of Dr Verwoerd designed a policy to give blacks Bantu education.

Verwoerd said: *"My department's policy is that Bantu education should stand with both feet in the reserves and have its roots in the spirit and being of Bantu society. There is no place for the Bantu in the European community above the level of certain forms of labour ... What is the use of teaching the Bantu child mathematics, when it cannot use it in practice? That is quite absurd. Education must train people in accordance with their opportunities in life, according to the sphere in which they live."* Lapping, (1986)

The problem is that we cannot wait for another generation of educated people to come through the educational system. If the South African economy is to survive and thrive in the face of global competition, it is important that we find a way of addressing the problem of the poor education of shop-floor workers. We have to find a way of increasing their capacity to understand the competitive survival issues facing us. We should also try to develop a collaborative spirit so that there is a shared will to survive and tackle the development issues facing us. We need to adopt a live body theory in training. This means that all employees are eligible for serious training and development no matter what age or level. The traditional skills training on its own will not be enough. Training strategy should be holistic and include generic education which should focus on the strategic and economic issues facing the company and the country.

11

The issue of civic education designed to educate the worker about patriotism and citizenship should be an integral part of the training strategy. The training and development should also focus on constant skill acquisition and best operating techniques as well as better work organisation based on teamwork and co-operation.

The training must aim at both horizontal and vertical multi-skilling, but even that is not enough. There should be a focus on best operating practices if the company is to achieve competitive parity. The reality is that most of our companies are not competitive. A wholesale skills upliftment on the shop-floor is an important managerial practice at the moment and in the future. Senior management should be evaluated on the achievement of this.

DEVELOPMENT OF CO-OPERATIVE AND COMPETI-TIVE PERSPECTIVES

There is a need to expand the perspectives of people working in African organisations to enable them to cope with the challenges facing their organisations. For African organisations to attain global competitiveness, they need to undergo a fundamental transformation which requires a total paradigm shift on the part of all employees. The underlying assumptions on which the African organisations are run may have to shift fundamentally if they are going to survive.

The shifting of perceptions and mindsets is the most difficult aspect of understanding transformation in Africa. What complicates the task is the inflexibility of attitudes created by illiteracy and the feudal aristocratic attitude of its privileged leadership. We need a passion to add value and create wealth at every level in the organisation.

In most cases, the capacity to understand survival issues is limited at both shop-floor and leadership levels in African organisations. One of Africa's major problems for example, is population growth and yet no African government to date has a population policy like the Asian governments have. The technology required to limit population growth in families is readily available, accessible and easy to use for poor families and yet poor African families have not been able to take advantage of this technology because of rigid perceptions in respect of family size.

The temptation is great for disadvantaged communities and individuals to blame others and circumstances for their fate in life. The reasons are often valid. The reality is that it will not change their destiny.

If we, as poor people in Africa, are to succeed, we need to develop a competitive spirit and attitude. We need to rise above our unfortunate historical circumstances. There has to be a determination on our part to survive and succeed in spite of all the constraints and disadvantages. We have to have this stubborn heroic spirit to overcome a feeling of being victims who are entitled to everything. We need to develop in all our employees, the hunger to succeed and the hunger to compete with other organisations in the global family.

DEVELOPMENT OF CO-OPERATIVE AND COMPETI-TIVE PROCESSES

A poor country which has very few accumulated assets can only compete through efficient transformation and production processes. The reality of poor societies is that they have very few accumulated assets except those that are natural. World-class competitiveness is a result of a careful mix of competitive assets and processes. The historical nations make it very clear that they succeeded by adopting and developing production processes that create value.

The management lesson for us in South Africa is that if our organisations are going to compete on a global scale, we need to develop unique competitive processes suitable for our people and market.

DEVELOPMENT OF CO-OPERATIVE AND COMPETITIVE POLICIES AND PROCEDURES

The challenge for organisations that are operating in a chaotic environment characterised by rapid change, is to remain focused on operational events. They have no time to reflect on emerging patterns and issues. The reality is that emerging patterns and events are a result of systems, policies and procedures. We therefore need to develop appropriate systems, policies and procedures. The focus on events can transform managers into busy fools. If there is no time for reflection, the reality is that one does not manage the opportunities, but starts to manage through lenses which only recognise crisis situations and problems. Managers start to see issues in terms of what is in the rules and their career interests. They will not be able to see opportunities and will spare no resources and time for opportunity management.

DEVELOPMENT OF CO-OPERATIVE AND COMPETITIVE INSTITUTIONS

If South Africa is going to be a prosperous and democratic country, it will need to develop democratic and co-operative institutions. There is a need for managers to democratise their institutions by developing inclusive and collaborative managerial practices. The problem is that a constitutional dispensation on its own can only create symbolic democracy. It is also not wise to entrust the preservation of democracy to the hands of a few symbolic and capable leaders. We need to entrust democracy to the hands of institutions which have the capacity to live for a long time, if not for ever. The issue of institutional innovation underpinned by bottom-up processes is a critical managerial issue for African managers.

DEVELOPMENT OF CO-OPERATIVE AND COMPETITIVE PRODUCTS AND SERVICES

The reality of the global competitive economy is that if an organisation cannot create value, it ceases to exist.

It is therefore imperative for African organisations to have a passion to create value throughout the organisation. It is important that the organisation not only meets customer requirements by creating user-friendly products and services, but that it constantly and creatively amazes the customer. For this to happen, it means that African organisations must have the courage to create unique products and services, never visualised before. African products also need to generate respect for "made in South Africa" rather than the current focus on imported goods meaning "status". We must become patriotic and buy South Africa. As Dr Kenneth Kaunda, former Zambian president once said: *Africa's economic problem is they don't consume what they produce. We consume what we don't produce.*

CONCLUSION

Ubuntu may mark the departure from the current confrontational approach in our industrial relations to a more co-operative and competitive approach of managing survival issues. We are not suggesting a romantic relationship between management and employees. We are suggesting a new way of forming a creative and competitive dialogue aimed at finding joint solutions. There is no suggestion that conflict will disappear. The collective solidarity of the various groups in the company should be respected and enhanced. The rights of these solidarity groups should be respected. Then the solidarity spirit of Ubuntu will have found expression in the management practices of our companies.

The dignity of our people has been emaciated by the indignity of Apartheid and as a part of the healing process of reconciliation, organisations should help restore this dignity in the spirit of compassion and care which are the essential elements of Ubuntu. It will enable organisations to perform competitively in the spirit of harmony and service. It is therefore important to understand the current dominant organisational climate or spirit.

The next chapter gives a framework based on the spiritual hierarchy of African spirits, which can be used as a metaphoric framework to determine the dominant values in a particular organisation and the possible values that the organisation can aspire to and incorporate into its culture in order to be competitive and adaptive.

CHAPTER

2

THE RAINBOW SPIRITS OF AFRICAN MANAGEMENT

We spent the night drumming and dancing
Singing songs of courage.
Was it not the last
We would be together?
When the ripening period comes
We catapult
Into the waiting world
Like the seed of dry pods.

I'm a Man by Mzi Mahola
From the *Anthology Strange Things*

Managerial reality is not objective and absolute. It is relative and culturally determined. It is a set of packaged solutions to complex survival problems. Some management practices are formed by the collective cultural experience of the people. Therefore, effective adaptation of management principles and practices in South Africa will only take place if the collective experience of the majority of South African black workers is taken into account.

The purpose of this chapter is to take one dimension of the collective spiritual and cultural experience of black South Africans, and use it as a symbolic, strategic, organisational and diagnostic tool. The authors of this book would agree that the

SPIRIT OF DEMBETEMBE

My spiritual route was firmly established when I was very young. At the age of three I was given over to my grandmother, Makawa. She was a reincarnation of the spirit of Dembetembe. Dembetembe was the Rainmaker for the VaHera clan who were originally from South Africa.

Dembetembe originally came from South Africa and became prominent in the first rebellion in 1890, called the first Chimurenga which means revolution. Dembetembe was a man and a cripple. The other participants, including a woman revolutionary Mbuya Nehanda, were executed by the settler government for causing the rebellion.

The role of the Rainmaker, in a tribal society, is to maintain an ecological balance between man and the environment. The Rainmaker is the moral conscience of the society in balancing justice and fairness. It is the checks and balances in tribal political systems. In times of political crisis the Rainmaker will rally people and play a leading role in removing the corrupt ruler. The people would then have to choose another ruler. The Rainmaker would never rule. He or she is above politics, she is also a soothsayer and intellectual for the clan. She would help to interpret traumatic experiences and emerging realities.

I was made a special assistant to Dembetembe and underwent extensive tribal, spiritual and political education. Most of the education was in the form of proverbs, story telling, folk history, games, songs and dancing.

African spiritual experience is so pervasive and deep rooted that it would be difficult for South African organisations to tap into this collective experience and align it with strategic thinking and organisational practices.

This chapter seeks to capture the spiritual symbolism of Afrocentric religion and use it as a dipstick for assessing corporate culture in organisations. The intention is to use the hierarchy of African spirits as outlined by the spirit of Dembetembe who was the spiritual leader of the VaHera clan of the Shona people. This hierarchy of African spirits tends to be transtribal. It would appear that she originally came from Venda during the early uprising and resistance against British rule. The hierarchy has therefore been named after this spirit of Dembetembe as a tribute to her contribution, since one of the authors was brought up and educated at the feet of Dembetembe.

Dembetembe was a "Gobwa", a rainmaker, therefore she was one of the highest spirits in African religion. The hierarchy is detailed below:-

The spirit in African religion is one's total being or soul. It represents our inner self and our total being. The spirit is who we really are. It is our values and our culture in terms of an organisation. It is the climate and values of that particular organisation and its very essence. We are using the African spirit as a metaphor to describe certain prevailing or dominant values in particular organisations and situations. The diagram below gives a summary of what each of the African spirits would symbolise in terms of organisational culture, values and climate.

THE CULTURAL VALUES	THE SPIRIT
Morality & dignity	Rainmaker (GOBWA)
Performance & enterprise	Hunter (SHAVI REUDZIMBA)
Authority - know the truth	Divination (SANGOMA/N'ANGA)
Power & conflict	War (MAJUKWA)
Survival of self & one's group	Clan Spirit (MUDZIMU/WEMUSHA)
Particular obsession, ability & creativity	Wandering (SHAVE)
Bitterness, anger & revenge	Avenging (NGOZI)
Cynicism, negativity & destruction	Witch (MUTAKATI)

GUIDELINES FOR PRACTICAL APPLICATION OF DEMBETEMBE MODEL

This model can be used as a dipstick of auditing the dominant cultural values in a particular collective manner that is in line with traditional African practices. This could be more effective than sophisticated and psychological surveys which the shop-floor workers have a problem understanding, which might also create problems with credibility because of cultural bias and a possible lack of understanding the interpretation of results.

Experience in using the model in running workshops with shop-floor workers, is that it is easily understood and accepted and used to extract dominant values. It is also easy to put across organisational culture to shop-floor workers and its significance in strategic management.

The Afrocentric religion is one of the few religions that does not look for converts; you are born into the religion. It acknowledges the validity and truth of other cultural religions like Christianity. In African religion it is considered immoral to expect other races to adopt our religion. People outside one's culture should respect one's religion. It must be made clear that in all cases Afrocentric religion has been used in a symbolic and metaphoric way to convey powerful strategic concepts. It is a shorthand that we use to capture strategic realities, using African cultural symbols. In the same manner, Charles Handy has used the Greek gods to illustrate key strategic concepts of management in his book called *The Gods of Management.*

Afrocentric religion does not worship idols, but acknowledges the existence of God and His role in creating individual destiny. As an African, there is a great belief in destiny. The model is also used to define current cultural reality of organisations. It gives a vision of where they want to go which is important for an organisational transformation for strategic management.

WITCH SPIRIT (MUTAKATI)

The lowest in the hierarchy of the African spirits is the **Witch Spirit (Mutakati)**. This is a spirit which is evil and wants to spoil everything on earth and in life. In terms of corporate culture, it is characterised by a destructive cynicism, indifferent and negative thinking. In South African organisations generally, the privileged groups are found to be cynical and indifferent towards the issues of change. They have become passive observers of their own destiny. This becomes a major problem in strategic management because the resource-rich minority have the skills, but their lack of enthusiasm for change, deprives organisations of the capacity to manage and sustain interventions such as Total Quality Management, Total Productive Maintenance and the Reconstruction and Development Programme. This type of complacent culture is also found in organisations that are in the declining phase of their development. It can also be a key feature of sluggish public sector institutions.

AVENGING SPIRIT (NGOZI)

The second spirit in terms of the hierarchy is a spirit which is normally good but has been wronged, and as a result harbours anger, bitterness and revenge. It is a dominant spirit among the dispossessed groups in South African organisations. Unless dispossessed groups can overcome their bitterness and anger, they may not be able to negotiate a **new reality** and a **new vision** in the new South Africa.

It is important for disadvantaged groups in South African organisations to overcome a sense of being victims, assert themselves and rise to the challenges of development and reconstruction and take ownership. They have to let go of their past. They have to forgive, not necessarily forget. We cannot change our past, but learn lessons from it. We can only change our future. The disadvantaged groups have to develop a will to triumph in spite of past and current obstacles. The definition of progress is the ability to turn a minus into a plus, a disadvantage into an advantage.

WANDERING SPIRIT (SHAVE)

The next spirit is normally a spirit of a person who is not part of the family, and is usually present in unusual individuals who have a particular obsession and a unique creative ability. It is a spirit of innovation. Currently, this is a weak spirit in South African organisations, and if these individuals could present creative solutions, which would assist South African companies in meeting the challenges they face, these individuals must be allowed into the companies. The strategic lesson for management is that innovative ideas for their organisations may have to come from outside their organisations and from outsiders to the system. This suggests a strong case for mavericks and consultants in generating new ideas for companies. This is because the insiders may be too close to the organisation, and therefore unable to see alternative realities. You cannot challenge a culture from within. It is politically dangerous and unwise. The majority of the people will not do it for personal career reasons. The politics of innovation and change suggest that the system will always fight back to maintain the status quo. In African culture, you are not encouraged to change the habits of your spouse. This role is played by a mediator, i.e. **Munyai** (go-between), or maternal uncle or paternal aunt.

These monitors, chosen according to tradition and custom, constantly come into one's married life to hear the unspoken grievances and to say the unsayable. Organisations that mean business with change and innovation should think seriously of creating a partnership with a solid network of chosen, reputable outside consultants whose role is continuously to change existing paradigms. In this way, the organisation can constantly create new ideas and escalate the capacity in that direction.

CLAN SPIRIT (MUDZIMU)

The characteristic of this spirit is a parochial self-interest in one's survival and own immediate group. It is a very strong spirit in South African organisations. Ethnically it is very important, so if the managing director is Jewish, Jews will find it easy to rise in the organisation, and if Afrikaans, he will surround himself with Afrikaners. The same way with the British or any other tribe - they surround themselves with their own tribe or clan. Due to the above, this spirit generates much conflict. If a system creates victims, it also creates aggressors and rescuers.

WAR SPIRIT (MAJUKWA)

This is a spirit interested in personal power and conflict. This is a culture which is characterised by power conflict and gamesmanship. The atmosphere tends to be extremely tense and the degree of personal insecurity is very high due to power politics. This culture is frequently found in marketing departments and young companies.

SPIRIT OF DIVINATION (SANGOMA)

In feudal Europe, it was called the divine right of kings. The key feature of this culture is that the authority knows the truth and if ordinary man does not share that truth, he becomes alienated and is persecuted. This is what facilitates one-party governments in African states.

The party knows the truth and if you do not share the truth, you could be imprisoned or killed. In South African organisations, management knows the truth and workers who question are victimised. South African managers do not want their assumptions challenged by rank and file. The majority of

South African institutions have spirits of divination. The problem in South Africa is that the next spirit is not present.

THE HUNTER (SHAVI REUDZIMBA)

This spirit is marked by a quest for pragmatic and creative solutions to survival challenges. Reaction in South Africa is slow compared to American reaction to disaster, for example.

RAINMAKER (GOBWA)

The highest spirit is the **Rainmaker (Gobwa)**, which is the predominant culture of an organisation. This spirit is concerned with universal truth, morality and human dignity. The challenge for Africa is to allow both the hunter spirit and the rainmaker spirit to be dominant in the cultures of organisations.

A key point to note is that in any given situation there will be two or more of the eight spirits (cultures) dominant. The dominant spirits decide the outcome and levels of energy of the organisation and then evaluate the ones which are missing and guide organisations towards those relevant ones as identified. For example, if one is going global, the clan spirit will not help very much. Some call this clan spirit the "laager" attitude. Some companies for example are predominantly controlled by accountants, engineers or lawyers. Diversity is important to ensure a rainbow culture to fit the rainbow global culture. It is also important to concentrate on positive spirits. In Afrocentric religion it is not possible for the positive spirit to exist without negative counterparts.

For the positive spirit to be predominant, one needs to separate it from its negative counterpart in a cleansing ceremony. The African practice would be to hold a ceremony near a river with a chicken or goat to be killed. The issue is not to destroy the negative spirit but to marginalise it.

In a corporate sense, one needs a corporate renewal ceremony in which one harnesses the positive spirits, through bonding, and marginalises the negative ones. One always needs the diversity of spirits to have the capacity to adapt. One gets access to the psychic energy of the organisation by crafting the relevant ceremonies and rituals. The idea of this spirit model is that each spirit gives rise to a particular or dominant characteristic of a particular corporate climate. The model has been used extensively with shop-floor workers and management as a way of assessing organisational cultures in particular.

The shop-floor workers relate to it very easily as it is not as remote as psychological concepts. It can also be used to convey the strategic vision that the organisation must strive towards if it is going to be competitive. It is easier to relate to than complex organisational development concepts.

After establishing the current reality of the organisation, the company is assisted in visualising the future state. A three-way sort is applied to establish what to stop, start and continue. Key players are identified who currently embody or personify these values - those wanted and existing. Those who embody the values one wants are developed into heroes by creating success stories around them.

They are then asked to tell their stories over and over publicly. It is by giving them visibility, that the company can create heroes. A company's cultural transformation can only be sustained and concrete cast through rituals, ceremonies and heroes.

The spirit defines and identifies the organisation, in other words WHO WE ARE, which determines WHAT WE DO, i.e. our actions. Before we know what we can become, we must first know who we are.

26

A case study of Eastern Highlands Tea Estates follows which shows how the spirit of an organisation can be transformed.

Chapter three is an attempt to show how undesirable organisational spirits can be marginalised and desired spirits enhanced using The Corpse Shadow Theory, which is a symbolic expression of the spiritual journey that the dead are expected to undertake in the process of becoming useful ancestral spirits or angels.

A CASE STUDY*

EASTERN HIGHLANDS TEA ESTATES

The important point to understand is that transformation is not just a search for better methods of carrying out what the organisation is already doing. It is about changing the organisation's being. It is about the death of the old ways and the traumatic birth of the new ways. It can only be done through myths, rituals and ceremonies. It is not just an intellectual journey. It is a collective social, spiritual, and psychological encounter. It involves the creation of new rituals. It can only be accessed through dances, song and collective story telling. This is what the case of Eastern Highlands Tea Estates is trying to illustrate.

OVERVIEW

THE NEED FOR SYNTHESIS

The first lesson that I learnt as an African manager is the severe limitations of conventional management theories and techniques in managing in an unstable environment undergoing rapid change. The limitations arise because of the time horizon imposed by management situations. Our workers in Africa want, in 24 hours, the material creature comforts that have taken other nations centuries to achieve. A further restriction is imposed by the limited financial, human, political, technical and social resources that face a manager operating in the African environment.

The task is further complicated by the diversity of tribal and racial cultural values. This makes management dialectic in nature. The challenge therefore is that of synthesising different

* This case study was originally published in *African Management: Philosophies, Concepts and Applications*, edited by P. Christie, R. Lessem, L. Mbigi as chapter 3 The Spirit of African Management pp 77-91

tribal, racial, economic, social, political and cultural values; that is, synthesising polarities of reality and stability, on the one hand, and those of vision and instability on the other. In the final analysis then, the challenge for the business fraternity is that of the synthesis of the economic duality of the feudal peasant economy, on the one hand, and that of a Western modern cash economy on the other. This was the challenge we faced at Eastern Highlands Tea Estates.

THE SPIRIT OF DEMBETEMBE

In my response to this challenge, as an African manager, I found the conventional Western management practice inadequate. I had to rely more and more heavily on instinctive and indigenous, tribal African wisdom and leadership techniques. As a boy I was sent to the rural areas to be a trusted assistant and guide to my grandmother who was a spiritual leader of her people. She was a medium of the SPIRIT of Dembetembe. The spirit of Dembetembe is responsible for the general destiny of the VaHera people. At her feet I received first-class education in tribal history, religion, politics and literature. I also received a solid education in morality, tribal custom and leadership. I received a tribal classical education through folk stories, poetry and proverbs. These contained fundamentals of our tribal philosophy. It was ironic that at the age of 22 when I went into the business world as a salesman and later an executive, I found myself relying heavily on my tribal education rather than on my Western education.

RELEASING THE HUNTER'S SPIRIT

SPIRIT

I received my extensive training in entrepreneurship as a child, through my grandmother, when I learnt to herd cattle, and also through hunting. In my culture, hunting is the major expression of entrepreneurship. It is a way of training and identifying entrepreneurs. It tests courage, persistence and endurance. According to the Shona proverb, "The forest only gives to those who have endured its harshness". Those who are deemed to possess the qualities of entrepreneurship are treated with respect and honour.

They are encouraged to venture into other areas of business. They are expected to be enterprising for they are said to have the **hunter's** spirit in them. The spirit of entrepreneurship then, is symbolised in our culture as the SPIRIT OF THE HUNTER. The particular individual possessing it is expected to be enterprising, restless, enduring and innovative. He is supposed to draw heavily on the traditions of hunters by having native shrewdness, emotional resilience, persistence, hunch, instinct, an eye for chance, enthusiasm, the capacity to work hard, to take risks and to improvise. In a way there is no difference between the feudal African hunter and the modern entrepreneur. They share the same attributes.

RENEWAL

In the African Shona tribal tradition, people hold frequent celebrations in honour of the hunter to acknowledge and encourage further achievements. Such all-night renewal ceremonies are called Marira, Pungwe or Madandaro. Pungwe means from dawn to dusk, Kutandara means to relax together. So during the Madandaro or Pungwe sessions the village meets all night for spiritual celebration and renewal. There is a lot of singing and dancing. Everyone who is present participates, irrespective of status, class, gender and relationship. A spirit of togetherness predominates in these ceremonies. The dancing, singing, drinking and eating is punctuated by the moral instructions of the mediums and elders.

BELIEF

My grandmother used to hold these in my honour as a young boy to celebrate and encourage my humble achievements in hunting and school attainments. She really believed that I had the spirit of entrepreneurship in me. She believed in me. This gave me a sense of hope and confidence in myself. She gave me that rare sense that I was someone special who was destined to make a difference in the world. This feeling has always been my companion. My grandmother used to say, "Although you are destined to do great things in life, always remember that the greatest gifts in life don't go to the most gifted but to the most persevering". She was a great teacher of entrepreneurship. I was fortunate to be her favourite student.

RELEASING THE COMMUNAL SPIRIT

FREEING THE COMMUNITY

The early Methodist missionaries and later all churches adopted the pungwe as a major evangelising technique. During the Zimbabwean war of liberation, the freedom fighters used it extensively as a vehicle for political consciousness and political education. The liberation `pungwes' resembled the traditional renewal ceremonies in that singing, dancing and slogan shouting by everyone present were the main ways of tapping into the emotional, social, psychic and spiritual resources of the organisation. They were also seen as a major vehicle of maintaining the morale of the revolutionary cadres and the peasants in sustaining the liberation struggle. The pungwes were also critical in communicating and sustaining the glorious vision of a free and liberated Zimbabwe.

RECONCILIATION, BUSINESS VISION AND COMMUNAL REALITY

When I joined Eastern Highlands Tea Estates (EHTE) the company's financial position was precarious. The industrial relations climate was hostile. There were strained relations with the then powerful Ministry of Labour and the ruling political party. There had been at least three riotous strikes. Morale was low. There was a crisis of expectations on the part of the workers. They wanted to achieve in 24 hours what other nations had taken centuries to achieve. Relations with the surrounding peasant community were strained and at times confrontational. The management challenge was very clear : **how to reconcile the workers' glorious VISION of prosperity on the one hand and the limitations of REALITY on the other.**

The way not to do it

Management's initial response was to dismiss the workers' dreams as impractical, to suppress and replace them with a more rational, informed and practical VISION. The workers were frustrated and they resisted management's practicality. In an attempt to accomplish its vision, the company appointed a personnel manager, a well-trained and experienced man, a former district commissioner who could even speak the tribal language eloquently. He was a true disciple of Western, rational, conventional management. Such a man was well qualified to inform workers about practical realities and to develop conventional management systems. The company had also hired a firm of consultants to help in the formulation of a strategy.

When I joined Eastern Highlands, the strategic document was not driving the company strategy. It was the daily management practices that were the driving force. Most of the executives could not remember the "Gilbert Report", which was the name given to the strategic plan. The personnel manager attempted to install rational management systems such as job descriptions, job evaluations, disciplinary codes and grievance procedures. He also tried to make sure that the workers were aware of the practical limitations and realities of the company. There was no place for dreams and primitive tribal systems in his management approach. He managed the company in a true sophisticated Western management tradition. It was a surprise that he met resistance, not only from the workers, but more so from his white colleagues. They did not fully support his initiatives. The industrial relations atmosphere was pregnant with hostility and mistrust.

The way forward

This was because the focus was on strategy formulation. The significance of FORMED STRATEGY or EMERGENT STRATEGY was ignored. The challenge of an African manager is not only to formulate strategy but, more so, to recognise the emerging reality patterns; what can be termed the formed or EMERGENT STRATEGY. In the rapidly changing Southern African environment, crafting or **moulding** of strategy is more important than formulating strategy. The Southern African manager has the task of conceptualising, synthesising and articulating the emerging strategic reality patterns that evolve from the synthesis of planned strategy and the reality limitations.

The introduction of conventional management systems met with resistance because the Southern African whites are a settler community, very attached to "PRIMAL", BASIC MANAGEMENT. In fact, the Southern African white community is regarded as one of the most enterprising in Africa because of its pioneer spirit. It is noted for ENTERPRISE rather than for conventional MANAGEMENT. The black

Africans, on the other hand, are known for their enterprise and visionary energy and the HAUSAS of West Africa can serve as a good example. The management challenge then for Southern Africa is that of evolving management practices and knowledge developed elsewhere in the world, to suit the African situation. Effective contextualisation can only take place if the African managers are willing to go back into their past and come back with answers to the relevant current problems. As Southern African managers we need to understand our dual cultural heritage, and honour and celebrate our achievements so far. The managers at Eastern Highlands were faced with the challenge of contextualisation in order to undertake the task of managing development.

REALISING DREAMS

I was appointed to turn around the situation at Eastern Highlands. It was clear to me that the conventional management techniques I had learnt at university were inadequate in meeting the management challenges that I faced. I was shaken, I was desperate. I relied on prayer and found myself relying on my childhood tribal education. I remembered that my grandmother on her deathbed had said that I was unique and would make a difference in the world. I came to the conclusion that the historic moment had come. The moment of truth had arrived. It was in this spirit and confidence that I resolved to transform the company. My historic vision and mission was clear.

I started to adopt traditional management practices, values and philosophies, consciously integrating them with Western management techniques and values. I adopted the traditional pungwe as a management innovation, as a major forum for communicating my strategic VISION, as well as for implementation. I did not try to make the workers practical.

Based on my own experience and the encouragement I got from my grandmother, I learnt not to discount anyone's dreams, but to encourage people to pursue their realisation, no matter how irrational they might appear. I encouraged the workers to pursue their vision of prosperity. I shared their vision. In so doing, I was able to tap into this vision and harness its energy into a powerful transforming force.

The pungwe open-air sessions were effective in raising business and strategic awareness. The major feature of these sessions was that there was full participation of every worker present, and the dialogue was critical of the status quo, being emotional and political in content. The leadership function was shared. During the sessions anyone could take on the leadership role. Formal leadership had a ceremonial role. The pungwe sessions were also effective in training, particularly in terms of changing attitudes to Western business values. The sessions were very effective in the creation and communication of a gripping corporate vision. The pungwe sessions improved morale and were critical in creating a new spirit in the company.

The new spirit and vision were critical elements in the transformation of the company. I communicated my strategic vision of creating a prosperous and enterprising community in the new Zimbabwe. It is my conviction that as Africans we have a right to prosperity. We have the power and a chance to create prosperity. I shared this simple vision with workers at every session. I felt enthused. Each session was dedicated to a primary theme. People would give a speech on their feelings on the issue. The discussions were punctuated by singing, dancing and slogans. Morale improved dramatically, and so did productivity.

CHANGING ATTITUDES

There was a major shift in industrial relations from confrontation to co-operation. At one point I got a call when I was attending a conference in Harare to come and plead with the workers to produce less because the company transport system and factories could not cope with the high levels of production! The pungwe proved to be a major strategic innovation. The junior managers and supervisors went on to incorporate them into their management practices. They held regular open-air meetings in their sections and at times I would share the platform with them. I had a monthly meeting with the representatives of workers and also with both senior and junior managers. I had pungwes with the school teachers, parents, nurses and village women.

LEADERSHIP AS AN ORAL CULTURE

Leadership has become an oral culture for me. The songs became more production oriented, the grass-roots mobilisers became more articulate, the slogans became more captivating and the thundering of African drums became louder. So the strategic vision became more dynamic and clear. The company was on the move. The informal networks became thicker and as important as the formal relationships. The transformation of the company was underway. It could not be ordered by formal edicts. It was a process which relied heavily on powerful emotions, hopes, vision and multiple leadership roles. Indeed, the transformation of a company is driven by a powerful vision. Rational management systems only assist. It is the spirit of the organisation, drawn from its historic past, but containing solutions to present problems and future hopes, which is fundamental to transformation. The pungwe sessions enabled me and Eastern Highlands Tea Estates to go back into our African heritage, and then come back to the present challenges of survival, offering both solutions and also establishing a living dialogue with the future.

DEVELOPING A "VILLAGE SPIRIT"

CREATING PSYCHIC COMMUNITIES

The resident population of EHTE is over 20 000 people. Instead of having large urban compounds plagued by alienation and violence (partly due to anonymity), we divided the residential areas into small self-contained and semi-autonomous villages. The idea was to create a true African tribal village in geographical, psychic and physical terms. Despite their smallness, the villages still had a fair amount of the urban problems of thuggery and vandalism. It then occurred to me that the social structures and institutions that are the bases of the village relationships were missing.

I then decided to create those social institutions that govern a traditional village. The common element in all the institutions was participative democracy and consensus decision making. Service and leadership were voluntary and unpaid just like in the traditional village. The idea was to convert the physical village into psychic communities. We created a village assembly for every village to deal with the general welfare of the village. This became the supreme board and its members were chosen by popular vote. Under it we had various self-governing committees, each with a single focus. For example, we had an education committee to deal with educational matters, and a women's council to deal with women's issues - particularly the improvement of women's education, social and economic status. We had folk choirs to recreate the company's collective experience into songs and slogans. There was a welfare committee to deal with welfare issues. There was a village court with the blessing of the Ministry of Justice to deal with civil cases. The health and safety committee dealt with occupational safety matters and preventative health of the village. We had voluntary "barefoot" doctors - that is, voluntary village health workers. These committees were self-governed and would seek advice from the personnel function. I began a programme called "Dandaro" (renewal). This involved eyeball to eyeball discussions, as well as training of these communities. It was a two-way educational process. We focused on the development of people, company, products, vision, ideas, relationships, communities, institutions, and the nation. The primary thrust was the development of harmony through the creation of collaborative relationships based on respect, human dignity and trust. These relationships were not unlike those on Robben Island.

The existence today of more than five preschools, viable adult education schools, a quality primary school, a viable health and safety programme and neat and attractive villages is a living testament to this developmental management approach. These are all run by the workers. The village model worked in solving the urban problems that haunt urban communities. The workers were very enthusiastic and embraced this indigenous African approach of management.

CREATING AN INCLUSIVE, ENTERPRISING COMMUNITY

After the initial success of the village model in managing the compound, we decided to integrate it with the conventional Western management systems. We developed effective consensus management systems through democracy, and through human care of the African traditional village. We did not destroy the existing formal structures but retained them to provide form and control. We balkanised or villagised the organisation into small semi-autonomous units and created a thick network of informal relationships that cut across the formal structures and relationships, to provide life and action that is so vital to strategy implementation. My vision was to transform the company from a mere economic entity based on exclusive relationships into an ENTERPRISING COMMUNITY with inclusive relationships based on the trust and intimacy of an African village.

Three of the key elements in the art of working together involve how to deal with change, how to deal with conflict and how to realise our potential. A legal contract always breaks down under the inevitable duress of conflict and change (DePree, 1989). Alexander Solzhenitsyn said this about legalistic relationships: *"A society based on the letter of the law and never reaching any higher, fails to take advantage of the full range of human possibilities. The letter of the law is too cold and formal to have a beneficial influence on society. Whenever the tissue of life is woven of legalistic relationships, this creates an atmosphere of spiritual mediocrity that paralyses men's noblest impulses. After a certain level of the problem has been reached, legalistic thinking induces paralysis; it prevents one from seeing the scale and meaning of events".*

ESTABLISHING INTIMATE RELATIONSHIPS

To **prevent** the alienation and exclusive arrangements created by contractual relationships, we emphasised the maintenance of primary relationships and eyeball contact with the workers. We introduced briefing groups. Every manager would brief those below him, up to the frontline supervisor, who would frequently brief his workers. The discussions would centre on establishing and reviewing targets as well as costs. This was done regularly and at times daily during the peak seasons. We also established the production committee to deal with production problems. We had a Workers' Council consisting of both managers and workers to deal with industrial relations matters, as well as a workers' committee consisting of worker representatives only.

The development of this web of intimate primary relationships helped to create a collaborative and caring atmosphere. This helped to synthesise different cultural values. Intimate relationships empower people to freedom and action, instead of analysis and paralysis. The intimate relationships rest on shared commitment to ideas, to issues, to values, to goals and management processes. These relationships enable people to find meaning and satisfaction in their work; they have the capacity to host an unusual person or idea.

We were able to develop people, products, social structures and a commercial organisation by having knowledge and insight into the development of African social structure, Western commercial organisations and African tribal society - with its emphasis on harmony and community care on the one hand, and integrated with the Western values of efficiency and enterprise on the other. This enabled us to adapt to the challenges of our environment through the emphasis on organisational harmony and collaboration and business interdependence. In essence, it is an African expression of the developmental approach to management, which the Japanese have perfected so well.

RELEASING A PRODUCTIVE SPIRIT

THE PRODUCTION FESTIVAL

This was my attempt to adapt the Shona traditional agricultural ceremony to modern strategic management. In the Shona society they have a production festival ceremony called "MUKWERERA". It is a strategic event to celebrate past agricultural achievement as well as a plan for the coming season. The ceremony is presided over by a rainmaker. I introduced the production festival at Eastern Highlands as a major strategic ceremony. I invited the chiefs, traditional healers, the mediums and the rainmakers, African independent church leaders, as well as political and government leaders to preside. The rainmaker led our strategic ceremony. All managers, including the general manager, would attend, as well as the workers, their families and the peasants in the nearby feudal economy. The rituals would be carried out by either the chief or the rainmaker, as in the true African tradition. The production festival took place on a Sunday. It was an all-day, open-air meeting, in a mass rally style. The workers could sing traditional folk and ceremonial songs. The songs would be adapted to our chosen company strategic themes at the initiative of the workers.

THE GILBERT REPORT BECOMES A LIVING DOCUMENT

The general manager and I would go over the company's strategic objectives and each pause would be punctuated by songs and slogans, designed to communicate and capture the company's vision. Cattle were slaughtered. There would be a lot of singing, tribal dancing, drinking and eating. The ceremony represented a synthesis of Western values of enterprise and Southern African visionary spirit. The result, in the case of EHTE, was the harnessing of the company's energy into a dynamic force to translate the strategic vision and objectives into reality. In fact, the Gilbert Report became a living document. The workers would be inspired to achieve the production objectives. During this ceremony the best workers were honoured and given prizes. They were called "production heroes". The best department and estates were also honoured and given prizes. The general manager and I would go through the company's performance during the year and the objectives for next year.

The production festival ritual helped us to unite diverse tribal and racial cultural values as well as synthesising the feudal peasant economy and the modern cash economy. This has enabled Eastern Highlands to tap into the emotional, spiritual, cultural and social resources of the company. The high expectations and hopes of the workers at Eastern Highlands and Africa must not be regarded as a crisis but as an opportunity for transformation. After all, it is the people's glorious hopes, fears, past heritage and dreams which, synthesised into a powerful VISION, can become the energy, which is the basis of any transformation. This has been our experience in Eastern Highlands. It has been an experience and a lesson in INSPIRATIONAL MANAGEMENT.

THE ROAD TO MANAGERIAL DAMASCUS

We learnt that management cannot be fully understood in terms of practical techniques alone. There is a need to understand the abstract, theoretical and philosophical aspects that have been neglected in the development of management thought. If management is to come of age, it has to give the abstract and philosophical aspects the serious attention they deserve. In fact, the development of the new sciences and fully fledged professions have shown that the depth of reality can only be captured by going beyond the concrete into the abstract, theoretical and philosophical world. Both the legal and medical professions would not be developed as they are without their value base. They show concern with their codes of ethics and other philosophical aspects of their disciplines.

It is my contention and experience that managers need a strong value base and philosophical base as a foundation of practice. This requires us, as managers, to travel the long road from Sparta to Athens and from Ephesus to Jerusalem. Management as a discipline is now in need of a ROAD TO DAMASCUS experience. As managers we need to enter a marathon race, from the master guilders of the medieval age with their emphasis on experience, to the Oxford philosophers of our present day. Complete reality and the essence of human experience can only be captured by going beyond the practical and functional, and by entering into the abstract world of ETHICS and VALUES - in short, into the world of philosophy and poetry. The management field has yet to produce its own philosophers and poets.

Visionary or metaphysical African management integrates ancient wisdom and modern science. My adoption of tribal leadership models in management training at Eastern Highlands can serve to illustrate this fact.

INTEGRATING TRIBAL LEADERSHIP AND MODERN MANAGEMENT

I started to use African tribal leadership courses for workers' committees, supervisors and managers. I would use parables and African proverbs, as well as traditional healers, folk singers, market women and traditional peasant farmers as role models for inspiring and empowering leadership. I integrated this ancient leadership wisdom with the scientific management concepts of Peter Drucker. The courses were effective.

For example, I applied simple traditional techniques, used by my grandmother in educating the young, to run a preschool education leadership programme. The curriculum was based on African playground culture, themes, folk songs and story telling. I preferred the illiterate women to be the teachers and trained them over a month, using action learning techniques. The teachers have been very effective and my own daughter is a graduate of these preschools. The major managerial task is to manage their evolution by interrelating ancient tribal wisdom with scientific techniques of developmental psychology. Mount Hope, a pilot school for children of managers and professional staff, represents such an attempt.

Visionary or metaphysical management of Southern Africa

represents a dialectic challenge to African managers of synthesising various polarities. The two major business opposites that must be synthesised are VISION and REALITY into dynamic energy. Ancient wisdom and modern science need to be brought into holistic management. Ronnie Lessem (1989) puts it more clearly. *"Placing particular emphasis on energy - that is its flow, velocity, quality and quantity - draws from a philosophical and experiential base that is now common to both ancient wisdom and modern physics"*. Fritjof Capra put it even more eloquently: *"the world view emerging from modern physics can be characterized by words like organic, holistic and ecological. The universe is no longer seen as a machine, made up of a multitude of objects, but has to be pictured as one indivisible dynamic whole, whose parts are essentially 'interrelated' and can be understood only as patterns of a cosmic process."*

CONCLUSION

RESOLVING POLARITIES

Based on my experience at Eastern Highlands, I can make the tentative conclusions laid out below:

a. The rapid pace of change makes the conventional management approach inadequate and calls for other management paradigms. African traditional practices and wisdom need to become the bases for management and institutional motivation.

b. The management challenges in Africa rest in a set of polarities.

- Stability versus Chaos

- Harmony versus Conflict

- Realism versus Vision

- Feudalism versus Modernity

- Freedom versus Control

- Diversity versus Integration

Therefore, it is a mark of African achievement to be able to balance and reconcile these opposites. There is a need to evolve management approaches which can synthesise these polarities, such as the four-world businessphere of Lessem. I have observed his four management approaches as a response to these challenges. The instinctive **primal management domain** draws on the traditions and rituals of ancient African hunters. The **rational conventional management domain** relies on the scientific heritage of the West. **Developmental management** draws its inspiration from the harmony, adaptability and care of the ancient African tribal village. The **visionary, "inspirational", metaphysical** domain of management celebrates both the spirit of ancient wisdom and the courage and dreams of modern science.

Of all the four approaches, I find visionary management to be the most appropriate in meeting African management challenges. It is capable of synthesising all the polarities. It can integrate ancient wisdom of the past with the modern science of the present, as well as reality and vision. It turns them into the dynamic energy which is essential for undertaking the task of transformation required, if Africa is to catch up with the rest of the world. The metaphysical manager is an inspirational preacher who lives in the grip of a vision and shares his experience with the organisation he leads and is seeking to transform.

"Each epoch and each society is rooted in some fundamental beliefs and assumptions which are acted upon as if they were true. They justify all other things that follow from them while they themselves are accepted as faith. A change in philosophy is a change in the accepted canons of faith, whether that faith is of religious or secular character; and conversely, when a given people, society or civilization is shaken or shattered, this calls for fresh thinking and a new philosophical basis. We shall need to create new myths to make transition in our society possible." (Henryk Skolimowski, 1981, **Living Philosophy : Eco-Philosophy as a Tree of Life**).

c.   The Eastern Highlands management experience is of relevance to mining and plantation companies as well as to managing rural development. The challenges of management require a new paradigm or mindset. Visionary management for me has proven to be an effective model with its emphasis on our past heritage, our present responsibility, and our dreams or visions for the future.

d.   The traditional African community is characterised by an organic structure in which primary and informal relationships are of great significance, as well as formal relationships. In traditional African communities ceremonies, rituals and symbols are of importance. These key features have to be expressed in the organisational forms that are being evolved in Africa. The new organisational forms in Southern Africa need to gravitate towards ORGANIC structural designs rather than MECHANISTIC bureaucratic designs. In essence, **the firm in Southern Africa has to be more than a mere economic unit and become a thriving, enterprising community as in the traditional African community.**

This has emerged in its embryonic form in mining and plantation companies without the help of purposeful design, development and recognition. Visible management, primary relationships, ceremonies and welfare issues are important in mining and plantation enterprises. These organisational forms can serve as a starting point in designing and evolving relevant management theories of the firm in Southern Africa. The new companies and managers in Africa have to be sensitive to welfare and social issues because of the poverty-stricken environment in which they operate.

Leadership, to complement management processes and systems at every level of the organisation, is important. Business leadership has to be obsessed with changing the status quo and replacing it with something better, but starting with an understanding of what exists and improving it. This enabling leadership has to be concerned with the following activities:

*   The articulation of a new direction and vision through the extraction of a relevant agenda.

*   The alignment of people within and without the functions and the organisation.

*   The persistent implementation and dramatisation of the chosen directions.

*   The recognition, study and articulation of emerging organisational forms and patterns as being important, rather than the superimposition of Western organisational designs and forms on African feudal realities.

STRATEGIC CHALLENGES

The strategic challenge for Southern African executives involves understanding the challenge of corporate and societal evolution. Many business failures are failures of evolutionary adaptation in classical biological terms. The major task of a senior executive is to enhance the probability of survival of the firm by enabling it to make evolutionary adaptations. A firm evolves from a pioneer stage of development to the differentiated stage and finally to the integrated stage. Similarly societies evolve from a feudal stage of development to the industrial stage and finally to the consumer stage, as described by Kotter (1990).

Business competition is Darwinian; only the fit survive. The definition of fit keeps changing and managing evolution includes creating processes for defining, achieving and preserving this fit. The major survival challenges in Southern Africa are as follows:

- Adapting to corporate evolution

- Adapting to industry's evolution

- Adapting to societal evolution

- Adapting to personal evolution

- Positioning within an industry

- Creating competitive advantage consistent with a chosen strategic position

- Understanding industry dynamics

- Responding to these dynamics or leading them

REFERENCES

DePree, M. 1989. *Leadership is an Art*. New York: Double Day.
Lessem, R. 1989. *Global Management Principles*. New York: Prentice Hall.
Kotter, J. 1990. *A Force for Change - How Leadership Differs from Management*. New York: Free Press.
Skolimowski, H. 1981. *Living Philosophy : Eco-Philosophy as a Tree of Life*. Viking Penguin.
Copra, F. 1985. *The Turning Point*. London: Flamingo.

CHAPTER

3

*THE SPIRIT OF AFRICAN TRANSFORMATION

Yet even at that final hour
My bleeding limbs may bend
To lift your cringing frame.
Against the bitterness of my pain
Perhaps you may come to love me then,
Though it may be late
And I will weep for both of us
As we   drown
                drown
                drown

Final Hour by Don Mattera
From the Anthology *Azanian Love Songs*

South Africa is continuously undergoing change while power shifts from white minority to black majority. This power shift is generating an uncompromising business agenda which consists of a set of strategic challenges that managers have to respond to in the appropriate way.

These challenges are as follows:-

- There is an uncompromising demand for inclusion and participative control by black workers which is a "kneejerk" reaction to the exclusive nature of apartheid.

* This Chapter was originally published in People Dynamics, October 1994.

• There is an uncompromising suspicion of business and institutions by black workers which generates the need to **establish legitimacy of management** and institutions. The effective response to these two challenges is social and political repositioning by establishing inclusive **structures** and **practices.** In Africa, politics is a megaforce in the same manner as the market and technology are megaforces in the development economies.

• There is an uncompromising demand for quality by all key stakeholders. The main reason blacks rejected Bantu Education was because of its poor quality.

• There is an uncompromising demand for performance by all key stakeholders, including emerging ones, e.g. the National Peace Keeping Force, despite legitimacy, only made one military venture into Thokoza and failed. It did not make history, it became history! This poses a major challenge for parastatals and institutions of the new government. They have to build the capacity to deliver in three years.

If they do not, their survival could also become questionable. The appropriate strategic response is to move away from professional and managerial prerogatives to **participative performance** and **decision making.**

• There are uncompromisingly high worker expectations for quality of working life and unless these expectations are managed by the leadership of institutions, it will create a major social crisis for South Africa in the next 18 months. It is imperative that management must deliver in both the private and the public sector. They must be seen to be willing to meet and manage black expectations. An attempt by South African managers to place black expectations at the lower end of their strategic objectives schedules will result in a very high level of militancy in the workforce.

• There are uncompromisingly high negative expectations of the **resource-rich minority** (privileged groups). The management of white fears is going to be critically important if South African institutions are going to have delivery capacity. If whites become cynical spectators of the new South Africa, they will be sabotaging its birth and become marginalised victims in the long run.

• The last but not smallest challenge is that there is competition for dominance and control in the South African marketplace. Unless organisations become world class and have a **shared will to survive**, they will not be able to meet strategic challenges. Corporate strategy for South African institutions is the ability to manage corporate evolution in the face of these changes.

The role of leadership in South Africa is therefore to be proactive and build the capacity of their organisations, not only to manage change but to shape the world around them. The strategic challenge becomes how to increase the learning curve of the organisations to cope with these challenges. Professor Reg Revans, the Apostle Saint of Action Learning, argues that if organisations are to survive, their rate of learning must exceed the rate of challenges and change that these organisations face. The purpose of this chapter is to propose an African spiritual concept of transformation and apply it to the management of organisation change in South Africa. The authors have decided to call this **The Corpse Shadow Theory**.

THE CORPSE SHADOW THEORY

Most African tribes in Southern Africa do not bury a dead body if it shows a shadow. A shadow in Afrocentric religion signifies negative feelings such as **guilt, bitterness, fear** and **anger,** which will prevent the dead person from moving on and being transformed into a useful ancestral spirit. The person then gets stuck and comes back to earth as a bad spirit.

If this happens in a burial ceremony, the mourners go into an open burning platform to discuss what exactly went wrong in his life and then carry out cleansing ceremonies to allow the spirit of the dead person to continue with the transformation journey.

The purpose of the burning platform is to allow the dead person to come to grips with his negative feelings and then to let go and negotiate a new reality and vision.

The important thing to remember is that the Shadow is being used not in a literal sense, but figuratively to symbolise the negative feelings of a dead person who is expected to undertake transformation into a new life. He is expected to let go of the past and be reborn into a new life with those in the world beyond.

APPLICATION OF THE SHADOW CORPSE THEORY TO TRANSFORMATION

The South African conflict and struggle have been centred around racial issues, in other words, our conflict and transformation are a polyethnic issue. Therefore for South African organisations to undertake the task of transformation adequately, the starting point should be an attempt to identify the various fears or shadows of the different racial groups in South Africa and then to enable the various groups to come to grips with their shadows emotionally and then to assist them to let go of the shadow. It is only then that they can negotiate a new vision and find a new reality. In the Afrocentric religion, in order to know **what you can become** you must start by knowing **who you are**. This cannot be done through a memo or privately, it must be done in a ritual and ceremonial manner. It must also be done collectively.

The organisation therefore has to undertake **collective education** by creating inclusive **open burning platforms** to discuss the gut issues facing the organisation.

The collective education and the ceremonies will enable the organisation's change champions to do paradigm punching and mobilise for **collective action**. Our experience is that these collective educational experiences ought to last two to three days and must be multilevel, cross-functional and multiracial. They have to be assisted by a trained facilitator, perhaps even input by reputable outside consultants can be given.

The weakness of traditional training is that you send an individual for training and he returns knowledgeable and competent but powerless to change the destiny of the organisation. The destiny of any particular organisation does not depend on budgets or strategic plans, but rather on how one harnesses the various self-organised **circles of influence** within that particular organisation. Unless one can enrol the self-organised groups and their key players in the organisation into the new vision, it is very difficult to change that organisation. Therefore, the most effective way to get through to them is through collective education organised in the "bosberaad" way. One cannot do this in an orderly, unemotional and sequential manner taking level by level out separately. These forums have to be inclusive. The act of transforming an organisation is a messy affair. In the African way, a nightlong ceremony would be held, punctuated by

55

music, dance and various analyses or consultants in the form of soothsayers helping to interpret and define the situation in the same way as corporate consultants. The ceremony is inclusive, i.e. including outsiders - all are welcome and selection is not practised.

This ceremony would be called "Dambe" and occurs when the spirits are being inaugurated. The purpose of the burning platform is to enable the various racial groups to get in touch with their negative feelings so that they can release these negative feelings by letting go and negotiating a new reality and thereby finding a new vision.

For example, if you want to introduce a best operating practice like TPM (Total Productive Maintenance), TQM (Total Quality Management), green areas or quality circles, it is important to have burning platforms first otherwise the new vision will not be heard. This explains why a lot of world-class initiatives have failed in South African companies.

There is also the danger that unless public sector institutions such as the civil service and parastatals are prepared to deal with the grass-roots grievances that have been there for decades, it might be very difficult for the grass-roots and shop-floor employees to hear about the RDP and to see the vision of the new South Africa. It is important that the various interventions must go beyond establishing new rules and structures and create space in open forums to debate burning grievances and define the gut issues in a collective manner.

WHITE SHADOWS

In our own experience as managers and consultants we find there are five generic fears among whites:

- **Fear of black revenge or retribution (this explains the purchase of tinned food and candles before elections).**
- **Fear of affirmative action. They fear this more than a black government.**
- **Fear of black anarchy or poor standards.**
- **Fear of punitive taxation or redistribution of wealth.**
- **Fear of nationalisation (the degree of public sector ownership is already 57%, so this fear is perhaps unjustified).**

What people should fear in Africa is the lack of public accountability and transparency by public leaders which facilitates the high degree of corruption found in African countries. The issue in Africa is not nationalisation, but corruption and "personalisation" of public assets by government officials.

The issue is not whether these aspects are real or not, because perceptions define reality. It's not enough just to adopt best operating practice. It is important that we must shift people's perceptions and perspectives. The challenge of organisational transformation in Africa is not about implementing techniques. The greater challenge is about managing the paradigm shift. Careful management of collective fears can go a long way in shifting paradigms.

One reason why things did not go well in postcolonial Africa, was the inability of the new ruling elite to identify white fears and manage them, by minimising the pain and loss of the resource-rich minority. The unique aspect of the **rainbow dispensation** was its emphasis on reconciliation and the management of the fears of the resource-rich minority.

"We enter into the covenant that we shall build the society in which all South Africans, both black and white, will be able to

57

walk tall without any fear in their inalienable right to human dignity ... a rainbow nation at peace with itself and the world", President Nelson Mandela: Inaugural Speech 1994-05-10.

The burning platforms will allow the resource-rich (privileged) groups to come to grips with their shadows and the depth of their guilty feelings, anger and frustration.

It is only then that they can negotiate a new reality and enrol into the vision of a new South Africa and the need to establish a world-class competitive organisation. These burning platforms will help the participants to acknowledge that the rules of survival are changing and will facilitate the learning of the new survival rules. This is an important **strategic breakpoint** which is a vital line to shattering perceptions and changing them. They melt mindsets and help to form creative chaos, which helps the participants to reformulate the problems and reality facing them.

THE SOLIDARITY PRINCIPLE (UBUNTU)

Disadvantaged groups anywhere in the world survive through collective consciousness and collective unity on all survival issues such as liberation, rent boycotts, strikes and mass action.

The authors of this book refer to this as the **solidarity principle** or **UBUNTU.** Individual conformity and loyalty to the group, is demanded and expected. The dark side of Ubuntu means failure to do so will meet harsh punitive measures such as evening "Dunlop treatment" or "necklacing", burning of houses and assassination. It is because of this solidarity principle that we find **five** major fears among blacks in South Africa:

- **Fear of being a sellout**
- **Fear of being sold out**
- **Fear of co-option**

- **Fear of white manipulation**
- **Fear of victimisation**

Unless there is a burning platform to address these shadows, it's difficult for change interventions in organisations in South Africa to be effective and sustainable. The blacks have come to grips with these fears in order to negotiate a new reality.

SPIRIT MEDIUMS

The other factor that determines the sustainability of change interventions, is for those interventions to find plant-level champions who are prepared to drive them. The element of individualisation is crucial in Africa where institutions and systems are in their infant stages of development. In Afrocentric religions, no idea becomes a reality, or no situation changes unless there is a human factor to personify and dramatise the change and the new ideas. This is referred to as the concept of the spirit medium. This explains the deification of African leaders in African nations. Another critical element is the ability to understand the prevailing situation and to change it.

This generates the need for guiding concepts or ideas which will be used to analyse the situation and formulate effective corporate renewal in South Africa. The problem then becomes that the South African corporate establishment does not respond to creative ideas and individuals. It has a tendency to glorify ignorance through the so-called emphasis on "hands-on" experience, which often means year on year experience repeated several times.

CONCLUSION

The critical role of South African professionals is to generate appropriate new ideas that can be used to manage the current challenges. For that to happen, both black and white professionals must be prepared to undertake inward journeys of self-discovery to find out **who they are** so that they can find out **what they can become**.

They have to accept who they are - **AFRICANS** - and abandon the neurotic desire to be American and European. The African intellectuals have to help us to discover our collective identity as Africans and help us to find a new collective **rainbow identity** as South Africans We need to search for and find a new collective **national psyche** if our development efforts are to yield positive results. We need to understand that the rules for competitive survival have changed. We need to establish and learn what new strategic rules look like.

We need to establish new **competitive** and **co-operative practices**. We need to establish **inclusive structures**. There is a need to understand our situational reality and yet remain open to foreign influences, but then adapt them into creative solutions for our survival challenges. The challenge for us in South Africa is to synthesise Western, African and Eastern managerial concepts and practices. There is a need to establish our triple heritage.

Our message is that the basis of empowerment has to be a positive organisational climate and enabling structures. The next chapter is an attempt to give guidelines of how this can be done in the South African situation without ignoring the collective solidarity of the black worker.

CHAPTER

4

*THE SPIRIT OF AFRICAN
EMPOWERMENT

It is long tedious
To some perilous
Some never get involved
Others swim against the tide
In their wisdom
Trying to lull its force.
It is a tragedy beyond words
When a patriot
Turns a traitor.

Road to Liberation by Mzi Mahola
From the Anthology *Strange Things*

INTRODUCTION

Although empowerment is a buzzword in South African business circles, there are very few examples of that reality in South African management. This chapter therefore tries to give guidelines on the infactuation of empowerment. In South African organisations the process that this chapter advocates must start with an inclusive burning platform to deal with all the concerns surrounding empowerment and to negotiate a common stakeholder, survival agenda. There is also a need to have an action plan with regard to the mobilisation of people and resources around the chosen common agenda. It is truly an Afrocentric approach to the whole issue of empowerment.

*This chapter was originally published in People Dynamics, January 1993.

61

COMPETITIVE AGENDA

It is imperative for South African companies to become world class if they are going to survive global competition. The traditional definition of competitiveness has narrowly focused on four areas of improving **quality** in terms of productivity and market share, quality, cost and innovation. There is a dire need to broaden the competitive definition to include the **relations** and speed of delivery involved in the process of wealth creation.

A world-class organisation has to improve both profitability and the social relationships of the workplace in such a way that the shop-floor workers can be motivated to produce quality products and services. The workers need to develop initiative and creativity, which is the tradition and spirit of the enterprising African villages. There should be management systems and values that facilitate shop-floor "grass-roots" empowerment to canonise the values of respect and human dignity. This is the spirit and cornerstone of the grass-roots democracy of African traditional communities and societies. South Africa's global competitiveness may continue to be elusive unless we can consult African ancestral spirits, through their traditions and collective historical experiences. There is a need to realise that any kind of organisational intervention will affect the power relationship between management and labour.

PARTICIPATION SCHEMES AND ELEMENTS

It is suggested that any kind of worker participation scheme should take into account both the prevailing realities and the collective historical and cultural experience of the worker. It requires management innovation that can capture and synthesise in a positive and empowering manner these realities of all the parties involved in the business transformation. The prevailing reality is characterised by political, economic, social and cultural diversity. There is a history of conflict and exploitation between labour and capital in this country. This has given rise to an industrial relations tradition of alienation and adversarialism which sees the interests of management and workers as inevitably and necessarily in conflict. Adversarial unionism and adversarial management can retard the improvement in competitiveness by generating paralysing polarity in the workplace, which benefits no-one. In South Africa we have conflicting visions of worker participation which enhance and sustain a hostile and fear-ridden industrial relations system. The system is infested with co-option, coercion, suspicion, mistrust, low productivity, exploitation and manipulation, based on a destructive zero-sum game.

It is the contention of this chapter that the reality of the workplace involves both **conflict** and **co-operation**. Therefore it is possible to find unity in diversity. The point of departure is the prevailing adversarialism. We must start by recognising the different interests of both labour and capital, then seek to synthesise this dialectic relationship. This means focusing on interdependence and developing mutual trust. This will make it possible for us to find community of interest through shared values and shared vision, which can be crystallised into a creed of trust. This is the essence and spirit of an African village and its moral base of Ubuntu.

It is possible to have both **graceful conflict** and **harmony** through interdependence and a common creed of trust. This is only possible if workers are empowered to influence decision making in a meaningful and co-operative manner. The involvement of the worker at shop-floor level honours the African communal spirit. It enables the company to harness its communal genius at plant level: involve the union at plant level through shop stewards to honour both the workers' collective community and collective spirit; and involve the union leadership at national level to honour the realities of political power and conflict in the corporate community enterprise. This chapter suggests a tripartite worker participation system which is both power and efficiency focused.

CORPORATE CITIZENSHIP

It is suggested that meaningful worker participation may not be possible without harnessing the African communal spirit of grass-roots democracy based on respect and human dignity - Ubuntu - as well as the spirit of harmony and service. Therefore continuous improvement teams (CITs), based on the natural working team and focusing on operational efficiency with the supervisor or team leader, should be formed. This will necessitate weekly prosperity meetings (forums) to discuss progress towards targets. The aim is to stimulate bottom-up communication and empowerment giving access to information, knowledge, training and shop-floor democratic processes. This involves capacity building at grass-roots level. This emerging shop-floor democracy will empower the worker to contribute to wealth creation and to derive job satisfaction.

The next level is designed to empower the workers collectively at plant level through their shop stewards. It also involves empowering junior management, as well as middle management. This requires quarterly operational meetings (forums) involving shop stewards, supervisors, junior and senior management to focus on strategic and gut issues of the unit. Lastly, there is a need to create a joint steering committee between management and shop stewards (transformation indaba) to deal with transformation gut issues emerging from both the prosperity and operations forums. This participation dimension is designed to address the realities of power and class interest in the workplace. This is the essence of business democracy.

UNION ENDORSEMENT

The third power-centred participation dimension has to do with the involvement of union leadership at national level and with senior management at corporate level. This can take the form of leadership forums on either a half-yearly or annual basis to discuss strategic issues facing the company. These suggested structures should be viewed as forums of co-operation to supplement the trade union collective bargaining. They should respect union territory regarding collective bargaining. It is suggested that the issues of political and economic conflict are best handled through the laid-down procedures of collective bargaining. The structures advocated in this chapter seek to harness the African creative communal spirit of harmony and service. They will not work in an atmosphere characterised by mistrust and hostility. The structures focus on interdependence and not on either independence or exploitative domination by any of the parties involved in wealth creation. There is also a need to focus on building a shared participative supportive culture and improve the quality of life of all the parties involved in wealth creation as well as optimise wealth creation. This is the essence of **corporate democracy**, but it must be aligned to strategic survival issues.

Embarking on effective programmes of worker participation involves four distinct stages and dimensions:

One : Awareness Stage

Management would start by taking their members through management strategy seminars, which focus on the imminence and inevitability of change in South Africa and the need for the company to be proactive for all business failures to manage change in South Africa. If, after the strategic seminars, management decides to embark on the change process, then a decision has to be passed regarding union involvement. The union and management, in joint formal and informal discussions, should access the timing, objectives and nature of the change programme. Strategy seminars involving employees at every level should be run to make them aware of change.

Two : Introductory Stage

A joint steering committee should be established and it must do the following:

- Clarify the guiding principles and objectives;
- Identify the capacity and training needs;
- Appoint internal facilitators, co-ordinators and the external process consultant; and
- Communicate the transformation programme to the total workforce.

Three : Education and Training Stage

Everyone in the organisation should go through strategic sensitisation seminars to identify the gut issue of conflict and co-operation, so as to come up with a synthesis of community interest in the form of shared values and vision. Change agents and facilitators will have to undergo in-depth training in managing the change process.

Four : Implementation Stage

The steering committee starts dealing with some of the gut issues and dislikes identified during the value-sharing workshops. The consolidated values as well as a code of trust become a basis for establishing the three suggested structures - CITs (prosperity forums), operations forum and the leadership forum. These become the embryonic structures which will be a basis for establishing the South African codetermination, which may be an ultimately worthwhile goal if South Africa is to be competitive in global terms. The change programme should then be monitored regularly by the transformation indaba (steering committee).

IMPLEMENTATION STRATEGY OF SHOP-FLOOR TEAMS

Strategy

High impact breakthrough strategy i.e. get measurable bottom line results in 6 to 12 months.

Process

PROCESS OF CREATING NATURAL WORKTEAMS

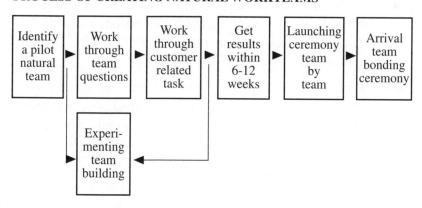

GUIDELINES TO TOYI TOYI
(Mass Mobilisation) IN SOUTH AFRICAN
ORGANISATIONS

- Select a converging gut issue or theme e.g. world-class competitiveness or non-racial company; RDP; high performance; TQM; TPM; war against cost; war against absenteeism.

- Set a best operating practice or techniques to drive it.

- Choose a pilot section or machine and have rapid results and high impact.

- Have a special launch or ceremony to put it on display. The team must choose special clothes, symbols (totemic emblems - "Chidawo") and mission statement ("Mutupo"). Everyone in the company must be witness to the occasion. Appropriate inclusive songs and slogans must be developed for the occasion. Rewards must be given to the team on the occasion.

- After the launching ceremony roll out rapidly throughout the factory section by section, machine by machine. Each section must have a launching ritual done exactly like the pilot.

- There must be a special clean and well decorated room for team meetings. It should have flip charts, overhead projectors and video machines. It should also have coffee machines and plants as well as furniture arranged in a circle.

- There should be a team building training and initiation for each team before its launch which must be repeated every year as a bonding ritual.

- The team must focus on the competitive market agenda.

The suggestion in this chapter is that the journey to world-class competitiveness for South Africa may not be impossible, but improbable without focusing on worker empowerment through union involvement and shop-floor worker involvement, both of which honour the collective communal spirit of Africa. It must also entail capacity building of the worker, shop stewards and supervisors by giving them access to more knowledge, information and skills. The point of departure is acknowledgement of our diversity and differences which are points of conflict, and focusing on the communal African spirit, with its emphasis on harmony, respect and human dignity, which are the points of co-operation. This is a basis for finding unity and shared community interest, which is the point of convergence, interdependence and co-operation, which in turn are imperative for wealth creation and not just wealth distribution.

CONCLUSION

Any scheme of worker participation must seek to transform the company into an enterprising community with freedom of enterprise. There is no recorded case in history where business succeeded without the support of the community. Above all, business success remains elusive if it is not rooted in cultural realities and the spirit of the people. In essence, there is a need to understand the context and generate the appropriate cultural concepts to capture the evolving business reality in the process of business transformation. South African companies must strive to harness their communal genius if they are to attain global competitiveness.

In the next chapter we try to outline how a company can undertake building world-class competitiveness through effective adaptation of world-best practices, principles and values by grasping the continuously changing competitive rules.

REFERENCES

Dekker, L D. 1992. "Toward Workers: Participation and Codetermination in SA". Conference Paper on Theory of the Firm.

Joffe, A. 1992. "The Importance of the Trade Union in Achieving Organisational Effectiveness". Conference Paper on Theory of the Firm.

Mbigi, L N. 1992. "Managing Cultural Diversity: The Spirit of African Management". Conference Paper on Theory of the Firm.

Maller, J. 1992. *Conflict and Cooperation: Case Studies in Worker Participation.* Johannesburg: Ravan Press.

CHAPTER

5

THE ROOTS OF AFRICAN MANAGEMENT

The only value of history is the basic lessons we can learn from it. Arnold Toenybee has stated that history is about challenges and responses. At the moment South Africa has great challenges which require extraordinary but effective responses. The starting point is to try and draw some lessons from the collective experience of humanity. The evidence from the successful, newly industrialising countries in Asia is very clear. Their success is as a result of a balanced synthesis of competitive assets and processes or practices. It would appear that the formula for success is as follows:

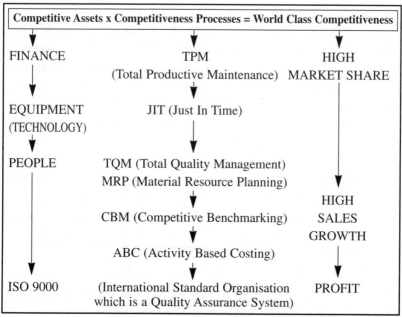

| Competitive Assets x Competitiveness Processes = World Class Competitiveness |

FINANCE

EQUIPMENT
(TECHNOLOGY)

PEOPLE

ISO 9000

TPM
(Total Productive Maintenance)

JIT (Just In Time)

TQM (Total Quality Management)
MRP (Material Resource Planning)

CBM (Competitive Benchmarking)

ABC (Activity Based Costing)

(International Standard Organisation
which is a Quality Assurance System)

HIGH
MARKET SHARE

HIGH
SALES
GROWTH

PROFIT

For business transformation to pay dividends it has to have a triple focus. It will need to concentrate on asset management in terms of people, customers, equipment and finance. In strategic terms, a major dimension of corporate transformation has to be about corporate restructuring and work organisation. It should go beyond manipulation of ratios and a focus on denominator figures. It should find a way of absolute increase in productivity. Existing assets perform better if there is a focus on process and work practices. This can be achieved through a focus on process re-engineering incorporating better work practices.

Over and above restructuring and Business Process Re-engineering (BPR), there is a need for strategic alignment and regeneration. The focus should be on influencing and shaping strategic driving forces. What we need to bear in mind in the third world is that one of the major driving strategic forces is government actions and the politics of desperation by various formations of marginalised groups. This is the missing element in the above equation.

If South Africa is going to meet the demands of world-class competitiveness it will have to be able to learn competitive practices and processes very quickly and be in a position to adapt them to its own survival agenda. The challenge for us is not to re-invent the wheel, but to learn competitive practices in the world and be able to implement them creatively to meet our own competitive challenges.

At this point the evidence is very clear that a variety of world-class initiatives such as BPR (Business Process Re-engineering), quality circles (TQM), green areas and TPM (Total Productive Maintenance) have not been a great success. The problem is not with the practices as they have been implemented in other countries successfully, e.g. Asian tigers and in the West. It will be worth our while as South Africans to question why these initiatives are failing. We have to alter the organisational climates by creating an environment in which these practices can be implemented. The tendency of South African companies is to reduce the renewal efforts to basic techniques and avoid the complexity of conceptual thinking required to make these initiatives succeed. As South African managers we are not prepared to deal with the complexity of competitiveness. We have a bias towards a shotgun approach.

In Afrocentric religion no idea or situation can be transformed into reality unless there is a totally transformed human being driving it. This person is normally called a spirit medium. The Western equivalent for this is a champion or a change agent. The starting point of corporate renewal has to be the deep personal transformation of the people driving the initiatives if corporate renewal is going to be sustainable. It is human beings who initiate and sustain systems. If the human beings have particular faults themselves, no best operating system in the world can work. The people driving the change must undergo a personal journey of transformation first before they can drive the process. They have to have a basic belief in the techniques being promoted. Extraordinary passionate commitment and discipline are required. They must strive to come to terms with their own lives. The extraordinary quality of spirit mediums is that their personal lives are a cut above everyone else's in terms of morality. It is not possible for them to give what they don't have. They cannot create change unless they themselves are changed. It is on this one fundamental fact that the success or failure rests.

The purpose of the change agent is to create a new spirit in the organisation which will make it possible to nurture and sustain the new practices. The spirit of the organisation defines what we stand for. It is our inner soul that will determine what we are capable of doing and sustaining. It will not be possible to sustain a particular process without creating the appropriate organisational spirit. The spirit will remain abstract unless there is a human face which can give substance to this spirit. The particular person is normally a very ordinary committed human being. The basic managerial lesson is that the starting point of introducing a best operating practice or corporate renewal is to look for the most appropriate spirit mediums and to facilitate their development by creating space for them to articulate new values and reality. The problem is that the current Eurocentric cultures and structures don't have a place for spirit mediums. They will find it very difficult to tolerate these obsessive and irritatingly strange individuals, who ask very sensitive questions and know no holy cows. Our proposal is that corporations must be prepared to alter their mechanistic structures, especially pay and grading systems, if they are going to attract such gifted individuals. Companies must also be prepared to give these individuals status and have them reporting to the managing director. The organisations must define the problems for these people to work on, rather than spending time on rules and job descriptions.

The other reason why contextualisation has been poor is because we tend to focus on the technique without changing our own paradigms and perspectives. The people with power in the organisation must be prepared to undergo transformation and shift their own personal perspectives regarding the world of work and competitive rules. It must be remembered that the Swiss watchmakers were doing all that the Japanese were doing, i.e. continuous improvement, research and development, but they had not shifted their paradigms of watchmaking. They continued to design a watch which would last 20 years and were not prepared for obsolescence or throwaway technology. A fundamental requirement therefore for managing corporate renewal is to assist the people who wield power in that organisation to undergo a personal transformation journey.

It is to challenge their assumptions about how the organisation is making money and managing its competitive survival issues. One has to use outsiders to challenge this perception continuously. Unless there is a perception shift on the part of key players, one cannot sustain new competitive processes. The other fundamental reason why our contextualisation is poor, is that we are not prepared to trace the history of that particular process. The African tribal concept of Nhorowondo will help to facilitate effective transfer of foreign management ideas and techniques.

THE CONCEPT OF NHOROWONDO

In the Shona tribal culture, in order to contextualise any concept or practice successfully, one must be prepared to trace its roots. This is called Nhorowondo. We are therefore suggesting that if we are going to adapt processes we must be prepared to trace their evolutionary history. We must try and find out who the key people were who developed that particular practice and what their agenda was.

- What issues and problems were they trying to solve?
- What problems did they meet in developing the concept?
- Under what circumstances did they develop the concept?
- Were the circumstances similar to the circumstances being faced?
- What are the differences between our situation and theirs?

We must then proceed to unpack only the elements of that particular practice that are appropriate and able to address our own problems. This should be done in a very creative way. For example, a lot of Japanese quality techniques were developed in an assembly line manufacturing environment. The extent to which they can be useful in other manufacturing environments depends on how creatively they can be adapted. One needs also to be familiar with the environment under which they were developed in order to adapt them to other environments. We must also realise that the mass production systems that were able to permeate every aspect of operations, including the service industry, have their roots in the assembly motor industry under Henry Ford. The mass production techniques in the motor industry gave rise to the current civilisation of mass consumption. The emerging world-class techniques also have their roots in the motor assembly manufacturing environment, therefore, in order to adapt these techniques to other environments creatively it may be important to be familiar with the motor assembly value adding process and to draw some of the mediums (champions) from there.

The champions do it as detailed in the paragraph that follows.

Changing the organisational atmosphere or climate can be done by challenging the assumptions of that company with regard to the competitive rules. This can be done through a process of collective sensitisation of top management, followed by the sensitisation of all the key players in the organisations. This is then followed by a critical conscientisation of the critical mass. This would help to shift fundamentally the perceptions of the organisation and create a climate which would facilitate the crafting of the newly found techniques into the organisation.

A good spirit or atmosphere should be created in the organisation to facilitate the change in the cultural heritage of the organisation.

THE SPIRIT OF AFRICAN MANAGEMENT

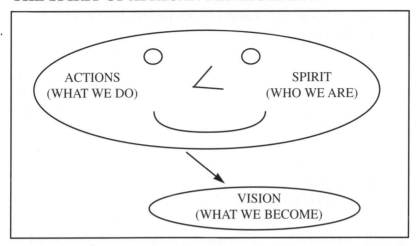

MANAGERIAL LESSON: BEFORE WE KNOW WHAT WE CAN BECOME (OUR VISION), WE MUST KNOW WHO WE ARE (OUR SPIRIT)

The starting point of organisational transformation is to understand the total being of that particular organisation. In order to discover its being, one has to go into its history, paying particular attention to its collective stories, nicknames, slogans, heroes and villains. These capture its values, and its essence. It is the collective stories in the organisation that define what that organisation stands for and unless that is understood it is difficult to change the organisation because to know what we must become we must know where we are. In order to travel to a particular destination one must know where one is. The impact of chosen strategic intentions and action is determined by the essence or spirit of the organisation.

For example social investment and affirmative action can only have high impact if the essence and being of the organisation have been transformed from the current racist climates found in South African organisations. Affirmative change is the basis of corporate transformation in South Africa.

This should be followed by a deliberate and continued education process with regard to the underlying principles and values of the chosen techniques. By doing this it will become possible for managers to deal with any breakdowns or problems in the implementation process in an effective way. To facilitate the implementation process it might become important to teach management creative thinking and shop-floor workers troubleshooting. All these elements of transferring techniques and creating world-class competitiveness capacity must always focus on the key business agenda of reducing cost, creating competitive rules. In other words, the key capacity required is to escalate the building of core competencies.

In order to transform an organisation successfully we need to pay particular attention to both the process element (the way we get the answer) and the content aspect (the answer). The dynamic integration of these two change dimensions is a critical task that the change must do creatively and carefully.

GUIDELINES FOR EFFECTIVE TRANSFER OF PRACTICES

The following would facilitate corporate transformation:

- Understanding the manufacturing environment in which the transformation techniques will be transferred.

- Identifying a shopping list of best operating practices and have a basic understanding of their evolution which would help in the selection process of the appropriate technique when this has been done.

- The next issue is to select the appropriate best operating technique guided by the history of that technique and the competitive agenda of that particular organisation.

- The next step is to define the market agenda specifically in terms of the other winning priorities and the "taken for granted" customer expectations.

- This should be followed by a creative alignment of that market agenda and the chosen best operating technique.

- Having done that, the transfer should now be considered complete.

CONCLUSION

The basic managerial lessons that we are trying to drive through the concept of Nhorowondo is that before a particular best operating technique is chosen to drive a new strategic direction, it is important to trace the history of that technique and then extract only relevant elements that address your particular competitive agenda. We are also arguing that change managers or those driving corporate transformation must look for an appropriate medium and be prepared to alter structures and ingrained systems to accommodate the champion. The recruitment guidelines should be talent and passion, and not education and experience. We are arguing that the people who hold power in the organisation and those who drive the change process must consider seriously the need to undergo fundamental personal change if they are going to sustain the change process. It is impossible to sustain change initiatives with unchanged people. The spirit of the organisation in terms of its values, principles and corporate mindset, should also be changed if the efforts in corporate renewal are going to be sustained in the African tradition. This would be carried out by an outside soothsayer, who will guide the particular family in its search for a new direction. The soothsayer has to be prescriptive and poetic and help the family to understand its current reality and paint a picture of a possible future. The soothsayer also helps to carry out the cleansing ritual and does the diagnostic work. This might suggest that if a company is serious about change it should consider, earnestly, the need to work with reputable independent consultants for a considerable period. It is doubtful whether a company can drive its initiative on its own from within.

In Africa we have to adapt world-best practices and technologies. The point of departure with the rest of the world is that our workers have limited education and life skills. The issue then has to be dealt with through creative human resources development and training strategies that focus on a rapid transfer of skills through the development of simple shop-floor systems. In the next chapter we propose an appropriate human resources model that is developmental in nature.

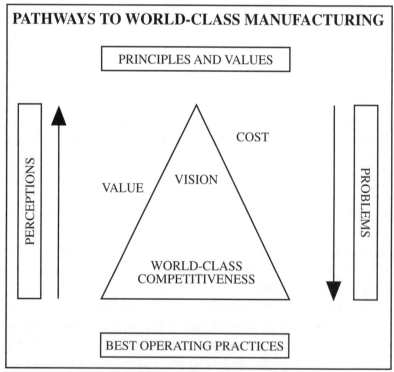

PATHWAYS TO WORLD-CLASS MANUFACTURING

PRINCIPLES AND VALUES

PERCEPTIONS

COST

VALUE VISION

WORLD-CLASS
COMPETITIVENESS

PROBLEMS

BEST OPERATING PRACTICES

NOTES: This diagram identifies the key elements required to undertake corporate world-class competitiveness.

The diagram overleaf gives the key elements that are critical in creating a world-class organisation - there has to be a collective shared view of what the situational world-class principles and values have to be. For that particular company there also must be a paradigm shift with regard to competitive and survival rules of that particular industry. In other words a shifting of perceptions and expansion of perspectives is a must. It is this dimension that will enable them to handle the complexities involved in managing corporate change. More time and money have to be invested in collective learning and education. If this is not done in the efforts of implementing corporate renewal the managers will not be able to handle any breakdowns and problems in the change process. They will give up and abandon the change initiative and consult the latest "flavour of the month" for guidance. The danger for managers who focus only on hard issues, such as the chosen technique, e.g. TPM, is that it will not be aligned to relevant change processes.

CHAPTER

6

*THE SPIRIT OF UBUNTU IN HUMAN RESOURCES MANAGEMENT

Remember to call at my grave
When freedom finally
Walks the land
That I may rise
To tread familiar paths
To see broken chains
Fallen prejudice
Forgotten injury
Pardoned pains

Remember by Don Mattera
From the Anthology *Azanian Love Songs*

South Africa is undergoing rapid political, social and economic changes. It is therefore necessary for the human resources (HR) function to redefine its role in the light of these changing circumstances. It may not be effective to transplant the Western management concept to the South African realities without real adaptation. Take affirmative action for example. In the USA it means: how can 90% of a politically and economically powerful white majority absorb a marginalised black minority which is politically and economically powerless? In the Southern African context, affirmative action has a seemingly different meaning. It means : how can a resource-rich minority

*This chapter was originally published in People Dynamics, October 1992.

83

of 15% whites absorb an 85% poor majority, which is currently or potentially politically powerful? The challenges in this aspect are different. Thus there is a case for the need for authentic contextualisation of management models in South Africa. Indeed, A. Athos et al (1982) were right in making the following suggestion: *"Managerial reality is not absolute; rather, it is socially and culturally determined. Across all cultures, in all cultures and in all societies, human beings are coming together to perform certain collective acts, encounter common problems which have to do with establishing direction, coordination and motivation. Culture affects the way in which they can be resolved. Social learning also establishes horizons of perception".*

In Southern Africa it is essential to adapt Western management concepts to address our own daunting management challenges. It will be the thrust of this chapter to try and present an effective South African HR model to fit our own realities.

ADMINISTRATION MODEL

It may be argued that before 1979 the HR practitioner in South Africa operated on an implicit administrative model. In the light of this model, the HR function is an extension of the managing director's office, responsible for maintaining personnel records and conditions of service. Its role is peripheral to the core task of the organisation, that of creating wealth, and as a result its visibility and status are very low. The role of the HR function will be advisory in this nature.

The major disadvantage of this approach is its inability to manage high levels of change. The changes in industrial relations brought about by the Wiehahn Commission in 1979, particularly the legitimisation of the unions of black workers, were too great to be managed effectively on the basis of an administrative HR model. The polarities, fear, mistrust and alienation generated high levels of industrial conflict and polarisation. This gave rise to a new HR model, focusing on conflict resolution and industrial peace. It is in this atmosphere that the current popular reactive industrial relations model was born.

REACTIVE MODEL

This model has enhanced the status and role of the HR function. Under this HR model, the HR practitioners are expected to play a decisive and visible leading role in industrial relations, particularly in resolving industrial conflict and maintaining industrial peace. HR practitioners have a policing role.

Its disadvantage is that it is forgotten when major conflict events, such as strikes, are over. The HR function operating on the basis of this model tends to have a "witchcraft" image in the eyes of management, a "sell-out" image and an "impimpi" image. Management does not see its direct impact on value adding and begins questioning the real value of the HR function. A minority of HR practitioners have started adopting a business HR model, which focuses on the business and strategic issues of the organisation.

BUSINESS MODEL

HR practitioners operating on the basis of this model see their role as assisting management to achieve their strategic business issues. The company loses its warmth and empowering spirit, leaving it with systems without passion, which retards strategic implementation in the long run.

The advantage of this model is that the HR function can make a direct impact on the bottom line, which enhances its status and value in the eyes of management. This can be very effective in high-growth and developed economies. The model is not feasible in the sluggish, slow-growth economies of the underdeveloped countries. These countries are faced with the problems of underdevelopment such as low return on investment, low productivity, skills shortage, illiteracy, a wide spread of extreme poverty and militant ignorance against value adding from both workers and management, as well as social polarisation.

It is for these reasons that the workers cannot buy into the business HR model. The workers will demand that the company - and the HR function in particular - must be sensitive to their poverty and suffering. Therefore they will impose a welfare HR model on HR functions.

WELFARE MODEL

The assumption of this model is that the companies have to assist their employees with their social problems in the form of housing and educational assistance, as well as health and sporting services. This model has a lot of currency in poor developing economies such as South Africa and Zimbabwe.

Its limitation is that it is isolated from the core task of wealth creation. It can also be abused by management to develop a dependence syndrome amongst workers and to use the services to exercise controlled exploitation of workers. In its most perverted form, this is paternalism.

This chapter proposes the developmental HR model for the Southern African developing economies which would focus on the issues of development.

DEVELOPMENT MODEL ("UBUNTU")

The assumption of this model is that Africa is a poor continent facing tremendous development challenges; therefore any effective management practices, processes and systems have to focus on development issues. No qualitative and meaningful economic, social and political transformation will take place without the generation of effective management paradigms. It has never happened. Any transformation must be preceded by a cultural revolution - the French Revolution can serve as an example. The HR practitioners have an intellectual role in their companies; that of interpreting the emerging patterns of a chaotic environment, as well as generating new models or ideas to guide the organisation as it navigates itself through our rapidly changing environment in Southern Africa.

The focus of the developmental HR model is holistic development. The model focuses on continuous improvement and development of people, products, systems, structures, markets, productivity and quality, as well as performance. The essence of this HR approach is a single-minded dedication to total development and transformation. Business and economic transformation in Africa has to be driven by people and not technological innovation, because we do not have the resources. Our economies are sluggish and the return on investment is low and unattractive to investors. South Africa's economic transformation will start with the development and empowerment of its people, as well as their collective efforts towards continuous improvement and wealth creation. This strategy can enable South African companies to meet the current challenges of change, competitiveness and development. HR practitioners cannot only maintain records and conditions of service, but must also create unity in diversity and optimise wealth creation, whilst at the same time remaining sensitive to the poverty and suffering of the workers.

Under this model the HR practitioners would be guided by four cardinal principles, to which I have given the acronym MIST.

M	= MORALITY
I	= INTERDEPENDENCE
S	= SPIRIT OF MAN
T	= TOTALITY

These principles have been derived from the values of the African tribal village community, which are essentially based on Ubuntu - literally translated, it means `a man is a man'. He is therefore entitled to unconditional respect and dignity.

- **The principle of morality:** The first principle is that of morality, which is the belief that no institution can attain its highest potential without touching its moral base. The purity of both motives and behaviour is critical to effective strategic implementation. This is best expressed through a passionate living of the code of trust. Public institutions in Africa lose credibility and effectiveness because of corruption. A good example is the South African institutions under Apartheid - they lost all credibility.

- **The principle of interdependence:** This is the belief that the task of optimisation of wealth creation in a world of want and poverty requires the collective co-ooporation of all the stakeholders in the enterprising community which can only be achieved by acknowledging interdependence. This is the superiority of the Japanese companies because of their focus on stakeholder unity.

- **The principle of the spirit of man:** The spirit of man recognises that man is the creator and benefactor of all wealth creation. He is entitled to unconditional respect and dignity. Man is the purpose of all organisations and they must work in harmony with him in the spirit of service and harmony. All organisations are present to serve man. When they fail to do this, they cease to exist. Institutions in communist Russia failed to do this and therefore no longer exist.

- **The principle of totality:** The task of wealth creation is highly complex and involves the attention and continuous improvement of everything in the organisation, by every member of the organisation: a building built by every member of the organisation. A building is made up of thousands of bricks. Therefore the building of a world-class organisation requires a thousand little improvements by everyone in the organisation. Every journey of a thousand miles starts with a single, simple step. The building of a great organisation must start with little improvements, in the manner in which we do our jobs, in terms of the improvements in five universal standards of relationships, quality, quantity, cost and timing. This is the essence of value adding. This is the essence of Ubuntu - collective participation of every member through freedom of enterprise is a precondition to the creation of enterprising communities in Africa. These five Ubuntu principles can simultaneously affect the management issues of co-ordination, communication, competence, competitiveness and compassion (five Cs). The current best practices e.g. TQM, TPM, ABC are based on the principle of totality or so-called systems thinking.

The role of the HR function, then, becomes developmental and strategic, but rooted in the spirit of the Africa-based human dignity and the creation of an enterprising community. The total transformation of the company cannot only come about through the creation of systems and structures but, more importantly, through the generation of new ideas. According to Weber, *"ideas become effective forces in history... Countless historical circumstances... cannot be reduced to any economic law"*. It was the idea of Protestantism that created free enterprise. Therefore it will be ideas that create the community. For it is the subjective values and romantic aspirations of the workers, rather than rationalised materialism alone - or the desire for community, rather than isolated selfishness - that are the basis for worker motivation. Therefore the HR function can help generate these ideas and values which can stimulate a wealth creation revolution.

The HR function must ensure that legitimacy is retained through grass-roots empowerment and participation, as well as creating processes by which grievances and dislikes are transformed into the collective action of wealth creation. The knowledge base will be mythology and the humanities, as well as social sciences. The political skills of communication, coalition and vision creation, as well as mobilisation, are also imperative.

The HR function becomes a transformative agent dedicated to the management of divergence and seemingly daunting changes. The HR function in Africa has to focus on issues of social, political, economic and business development as they assert themselves in the company and the African business environment.

CONCLUSION

The new HR person will have to be far more integrated into the business and with other managerial functions, especially operations. They must have a deep understanding of production, marketing and finance so as to assist the organisation to overcome its performance problem through the systematic development of best practices. The HR function in Southern Africa has a developmental and strategic role. The essence of strategic management is to create the capacity of a company to cope with the challenges of a rapidly changing environment. It must be remembered that all business failures are failures to adapt to changing external and internal circumstances. Today's major competitive edge is the company's ability to implement its strategic thrusts with speed. The HR function has to assist companies to create cultures of velocity.

One way to do this is through empowerment, by opening access to wealth creation, knowledge and participative processes, particularly at grass-roots level. This will not only facilitate speed of implementation, but also minimise the pain and loss generated by change. Secondly, it will enable the company to harness its diversity into a creative, value-adding force. This, in turn, will enhance the company's capacity to continuously improve and adapt through the generation of a variety of ideas. Variety is the spice of life, according to Pascale, *"For any system to adapt to its external environment, its internal controls must incorporate variety. If one reduces variety inside, a system is unable to cope with variety outside. The innovative organisation must incorporate variety into its processes"*.

Thirdly, this can enhance the company's discernment ability by being rooted in African realities and triple-cultural heritage, i.e. our Western, colonial and tribal heritage. In short, the basis of effective strategic management in South Africa is effective people management and the restoration of their dignity through their development and empowerment.

In the next chapter we try to show how South African companies can develop racial and cultural diversity to ensure adaptive survival in the changing social, political and economic circumstances.

REFERENCES

Athos, A. *et al.* 1982. *Interpersonal Behavior*. Englewood Cliffs, New Jersey: Prentice Hall.

Lessem, R. 1987. *The Global Business*. London: Prentice Hall.

Mbigi L N. 1991. "Managing Cultural Diversity: The Spirit of African Management" Conference Paper: Ashridge Management College, U.K.

Pascale, R T *et al.* 1989. *The Art of Japanese Management*. London: Penguin Books.

Pascale, R. 1990. *Managing on the Edge : How Successful Companies Use Conflict to Stay Ahead*. London: Penguin.

CHAPTER

7

AFFIRMATIVE ACTION : AN APPROPRIATE AFROCENTRIC APPROACH

The extent to which the current political dispensation will be successful will depend on management of the high expectations of the black population for improved quality of life on the one hand, and the white negative fears on the other hand. The central issue to these two separate agendas is the distribution of opportunities, resources and status. At the heart of the debate is what the emerging public policy will be. How will it address past imbalances and inequalities? In other words, the issue of affirmative action and how it will be managed will determine the success of the current efforts at nation building in South Africa. It is for this reason that it is very important to clarify the issues and challenges related to the topic of affirmative action. The last word on affirmative action is yet to be written.

The intention of this chapter is not to resolve the issues related to affirmative action, but to clarify and stimulate debate on the topic. The key point that the authors would like to focus on is the need to contextualise affirmative action in order to move away from an American approach, to a more appropriate Afrocentric approach to the issue. In the USA affirmative action is about the integration of a marginalised black minority which is politically and economically powerless with a 90% white majority, which is politically and economically powerful. In fact, if in America this ten percent was promoted into

93

managerial and supervisory positions, it would not substantially alter the material circumstances of the white majority and their life opportunities.

In South Africa, the context is different and this gives affirmative action a different meaning to both blacks and whites. How can a resource minority of 15% whites with a threatened power base absorb an 85% poverty-stricken majority, which is politically powerful? The challenges in this aspect are very different. It is therefore imperative for us to define a new meaning for affirmative action and develop Afrocentric strategies for implementing it.

The starting point is to identify the key issues involved in affirmative action in South Africa and what the guiding principles in dealing with those key issues will be.

What is very clear is that affirmative action in South Africa is not about correcting demographic imbalances, but about appropriate actions to deal with major societal restructuring. In fact, at the heart of the whole issue is the debate about what kind of society the new South Africa should be like. What kind of institutions should be created? It is a debate that is about large-scale normative change and the appropriate public policy actions that should be undertaken as well as company actions to be carved out by managers.

We therefore need a wider and more comprehensive perspective with regard to affirmative action.

KEY ISSUES IN AFFIRMATIVE ACTION

The following are the key issues that need to be addressed in dealing with affirmative action at both government and company level.

- **The Principle of Transparency and Accountability**

  It is important that affirmative action policy must require disclosure of relevant information and insist on the accountability of those who make decisions.

- **The Principle of Partnership with Black Business and Vendors**

  The need for partnerships with black business cannot be overemphasised. The blacks as a racial group in South Africa own less than 4% of the national assets in this country and therefore black economic empowerment should be an important aspect of any affirmative action policy at both government and company level. This would necessitate joint business ventures with black businessmen. It would also necessitate employee share ownership as well as subcontraction to black vendors.

- **The Principle of Inclusivity**

  There will be a need for inclusive corporate governance. This will necessitate the creation of participative structures with legitimate stakeholders at plant level to deal with company performance and joint management teams or counsels. It would also necessitate the appointment of black and union directors on company boards.

- ## Black Managers and Directors in Decision Making Structures

  There is a greater need for the appointment of black managers in the management structure into meaningful staff and line positions in which they control resources, i.e. budgets, information, cheque-signing authority. The blacks must also have strong representation on key company committees such as the Capex committee, the staff development committee, the budget committee.

- ## Worker Empowerment

  Affirmative action needs to be truly comprehensive and target every black employee in the company and not just the black elite. It should involve the empowerment of shop-floor workers not only in terms of decision making, but also in terms of constant skill acquisition. The development of workers should include the regrading of workers and revisiting of job evaluation which means that jobs are not evaluated on the basis of task, but on the basis of skill. The job evaluation must strive to reduce the variance levels to a maximum of 6 grades. Broadbanding becomes an important issue. Career pathing, vertical multiskilling and recognition of prior learning is very important. It is also important to recognise ongoing training on the job so as to make the skills portable throughout the industry, and also for greater employability. Payment for skills becomes an important aspect of training and development. It is important that the collective voice of all the stakeholders must be involved in skills development and design and implementation of the programme. The legacy of Apartheid has left very high levels of illiteracy and very low levels of life skills, which need to be addressed through a dynamic adult education programme. It is

96

only through this action that the worker can feel empowered.

- **Accelerated Development and Mobility**

  One has to appreciate the impatience in the black community to get their own liberation dividend, so if affirmative action programmes are to be credible to the blacks then there must be accelerated training and development which involves coaching and a serious intention to appoint them to immediate positions either as designates or in the position. The idea is to avoid trainee and understudy positions. It is difficult for a manager to train his own successor. There is a possibility if the manager is white, that the black trainee who is appointed will never be ready, in his eyes.

- **Afrocentric World View**

  The hallmark of Afrocentric philosophy is about being a good community member. It is also about living and enjoying life rather than the acquisition of the material creature comforts of life. It is about accepting one's destiny rather than an obsession to control it. It is not about controlling results, but about expecting and living with the outcome.

There is also the principle of inclusivity which requires that those most affected by discrimination, such as black trade unions and staff associations, should be involved in designing and implementing the affirmative action process. The company should show its commitment to the affirmative action process by having a very clear policy on the topic with specific targets driven from the corporate MD's office. It is important that they should be incorporated into the national budgeting process and management should be evaluated on affirmative action targets.

The reality in South African management is that if it is not measured, it is ignored.

THE NEED FOR AFFIRMATIVE CHANGE

Our experience is that affirmative action will not work without affirmative change. The company must be prepared to address the whole company climate. There is a need to create a new culture of tolerance and respect for **political, racial, tribal, religious** and **cultural** diversity. It has to be a total effort, applicable to all levels from shop-floor to boardroom. The issues related to cultural tolerance tend to be emotional. We therefore strongly recommend the continuous involvement of reputable outside consultants and third parties.

It is difficult in a divided society for racial attitudes to be sufficiently challenged from within. The commitment reality of South Africa is that we are still a divided society because we spent over half a century emphasising our differences. The struggle and conflict in South Africa is about finding each other. It is an implosion of human similarities. Human beings are complex creatures. They are both similar and dissimilar. Effective human existence requires us to acknowledge this complexity. In the old Russian Soviet empire they did the opposite - they imposed similarities and today Russia is faced with an explosion of differences.

The efforts of corporate cultural transformation in South Africa must encourage acceptance of our differences and the discovery of our similarities. The process must avoid emphasising differences, e.g. Zulus accept you one way and Xhosas another way. The processes must emphasise similarities and the creation of a common survival agenda. Therefore the emancipating African concept of Ubuntu is of great significance with its emphasis on human dignity, respect and collective unity. Ubuntu could facilitate the development of an inclusive national and corporate vision based on compassion and tolerance as well as the will to survive in spite of the constraints of our history.

Most successful cultural transformation programmes require a sustained effort of 3 - 5 years and part of the experience tends to be off site and residential. It also requires the creation of appropriate company rituals and ceremonies designed to foster social bonding (see Mass Mobilisation guidelines in Chapter 4). It is hard to create a new culture through seminars alone or through training and development plans, which are in reality menus. We need to create social encounters which will put the advocated values on constant display. We also feel that there must be careful strategic alignment, which leads to the development of a collective common survival and competitive agenda, otherwise the transformation initiative becomes stale.

CONCLUSION

The emerging Afrocentric definition on affirmative action is very comprehensive. It is about the appropriate action required to create a nonracial, democratic society and its institutions. This can only happen through a careful, passionate leadership alliance with other stakeholders far beyond the boundaries of any company. It will require public policy development and monitoring as well as corporate leadership that is bold and innovative and can see the big picture on a long-term basis. The investment is now, but the return will come much later.

The next chapter will discuss some important elements of leadership. Leadership is going to be crucial if the new South Africa is going to be established. The appropriate leadership style is largely dictated by cultural imperatives. The time has come to try and articulate the emerging Afrocentric leadership model with its emphasis on visibility and constituent sensitivity as well as service.

CHAPTER

8

THE CULTURAL DIMENSIONS OF TRANSFORMATION

His baby cry
was of a cub
tearing the neck
of the lioness
because he was fatherless.

The gods ...
boiled his blood
in a clay pot of passion
to course in his veins.

His heart was shaped into an ox shield
to foil every foe.

Ancestors forged
his muscles into
thongs as tough
as wattle bark
and nerves
as sharp as
syringa thorns.

His eyes were lanterns
that shone from the dark valleys of Zululand
to see white swallows
coming across the sea.
His cry to two assassin brothers:

Ubuntu

> *"Lo! You can kill me*
> *but you'll never rule this land!"*

The Birth of Shaka by Oswald Mbuyiseni Mtshali
from *Poems of Black Africa*

Change is influenced by cultural circumstances. It reflects the cultural possibilities and constraints that the activists of change have to deal with. These cultural roots influence the focus and type of effective change processes which will ensure that we deal with the abovementioned change in the best possible way. It is not easy to draw neat little boxes of each culture, but the authors are merely commenting. The cultural perceptions define who we are and our reality. It is our world!

ATTITUDE TO CHANGE

If one just looks at different cultural perspectives on change, this can help one to understand how different cultural groups respond to change. Take the British versus the Americans for example. The British believe in tradition. Their attitude is - so why change it? British also believe in individual freedom, which has been the source of innovation in the British society.

In British society individual freedom is sacrosanct. Change must therefore come from the individual and organisations must create the space for him. Society goes about its business as usual according to tradition. Britain is the only country with an unwritten constitution.

The Americans, on the other hand, believe that anything new is good. Old things are treated with a certain irreverence as something better is always around the corner.

The Afrocentric view is a belief in destiny and this belief in destiny has helped to foster an adaptation to the dramatic aspects of change which has been very beneficial. It helps us to cope with the desperate conditions in we find ourselves in Africa.

It has meant that choice has also been handled along the same lines as above whereas Americans are very different. Destiny does not come into it, leaders you cannot change make them nervous. Limited choice makes them nervous. On the other hand the British are far more complacent about choice, happy when someone else is in charge and they know what is expected of them.

ATTITUDE TO REWARD

When planning a change process one is constantly thinking of ways to introduce milestones during the change process so that steps of progress are celebrated and people are rewarded differently depending on the "audience", i.e. depending on those involved in the change process. For example, you bring in some type of incentives scheme for a team-based activity. The Americans would see this "money" as a measure of success and the final guarantee that choices made were the "right" ones.

The British, however, would see this "money" as vulgar and undermining the human spirit. Haggling about money is okay for the shop-floor workers, but others must concern themselves with loyalty to the employer. The concept of higher-level employees being involved in "additional" rewards is foreign.

The Afrocentric view of rewards is based on Ubuntu. One works for additional reward so that one's fellow man can enjoy the fruits of one's labour. Whatever one earns is for the collective good of the community.

Ubuntu

ATTITUDE TO TEAM

Many change processes are based on forming work teams, which will conclude tasks with the objective of achieving change, which will contribute to a greater change goal.

Take different cultural perspectives on teamwork. The Americans believe that if each person concentrates on attaining his personal best and achieving inner fulfilment, this automatically contributes to the team's greater good, whereas the British feel that if they threw down the gauntlet and said, " I come first" this would be notification of battle. Similarly, in the Afrocentric view one thinks in terms of collective survival. Group loyalty is the key issue in building a team.

ATTITUDE TO CHANGE MANAGEMENT

People's cultural collective experience influences the focus and type of effective change interventions. Experience with American organisations is that the focus of transformative efforts is on developing **leadership capacity and models**. This may be due to the American frontier and pioneer experience and spirit. There is a sincere search for a leadership formula in America. The leaders tend to be both mythical and real. The role of a change consultant in America is that of enabling the organisation to develop both **real** and **mythical heroic** leaders. The consultant of necessity helps the organisation to define the type of leader and his role. The American audience displays gangster tendencies - they seem to want two major types of leadership: **inspiring visionary** and **enterprising visionary.** The leader has to be messianic, articulate and powerful enough to lead his people from the current Egypt of suffering to Canaan of their dreams. They love courage and action, action and action.

The focus on managing change for European organisations is

on creating enabling structures which can give space to the individual so that he can be more innovative. The role of a change consultant is to help organisations develop facilitating bottom-up structures including hierarchical and parallel organisations. The consultant must also enable both managers and individual employees to define their new **roles, relationships and responsibilities** (3Rs), as well as helping individuals to develop their relevant skills. The focus is on building individual competence and self-reliance.

In Eastern countries the focus of change management tends to be the creation of appropriate organisational processes. The role of a change consultant is to help the organisation to create these processes. For Eastern organisations in particular it is the creation of teamwork and the creation of corporate culture that emphasise the importance of **doing together** (teamwork).

In Mother Africa focus on change efforts has to be creation of harmony between the individual and his **community** as well as nature, particularly **ancestral spirits**. The survival challenges in feudal underdeveloped society that has not conquered nature are terrifying. The question of **freedom of choice** for the individual is out; what is crucial is **freedom from want**. It is also theoretical nonsense to expect individual self-reliance and independence. One survives by joining hands with others. South African organisations like the Zionist Christian churches survive on the bases of the **solidarity principle** and **absolute group conformity** on survival issues. This is their competitive edge. Maybe this is what gave birth to and sustained the South African primitive political ideology of Apartheid based on race and group commandment. The focus of change interventions will have to aim at total community upliftment and mobilisations. In companies the focus should be on the mobilisation of the shop-floor workers and their upliftment and empowerment.

CONCLUSION

The decisive difference in terms of corporate revitalisation only comes when one starts focusing change efforts in the total workforce and the development of animating and facilitating grass-roots leadership through personal empowerment and collective education programmes. Leadership in Africa has to be servant leadership, which is visible, symbolic and articulate in terms of face to face communication in mass rally style.

Leadership in South Africa is an oral culture; the use of symbols, dances, songs and rituals such as mass meetings are important ways of gaining access to the emotional and psychic energy of the organisation. African organisations and people can transcend the tragic situations of their environments through an unyielding faith in those in the world beyond (ancestral spirits).

The role of a change consultant in Africa is that of an animating enabler and a translator of complex concepts into elementary ideas so that they can be readily understood by simple semi-illiterate shop-floor workers. The consultant must also be a soothsayer who interprets the dynamics of change and situations to simple shop-floor workers in a manner readily understood by a feudal community. (The aim is to develop a collective shared will to survive in spite of the constraints and obstacles of development.) The tasks of change agents in South Africa is to help transform companies from being alienating economic units into enterprising communities (villages) in order to optimise wealth creation. In a society characterised by racial divisions, poverty and suffering, this can be a noble and inspiring task. Cultural dimensions seem to have a significant impact on the management of transformation.

The role of leadership and consultants in Africa is to develop unique approaches to the challenge of reconstruction and development. The next chapter addresses this issue in respect of people development.

CHAPTER

9

UBUNTU: THE AFRICAN SPIRIT OF COLLECTIVE DEVELOPMENT AND RECONSTRUCTION IN ORGANISATIONS

"Chara chimive hachitswane inda"

African Shona Proverb

A thumb working on its own is useless. It has to work collectively with the other fingers to get strength and be able to achieve anything.

The essence of Ubuntu is collective shared experience and the collective solidarity. This has serious implications for the development of people and organisations. The traditional training and development approaches may be very marginal and of peripheral relevance to the development of people and organisations in Africa.

Traditional approaches tend to be truncated and focus on the individual. If you send an executive off to a seminar on his own he will become very knowledgeable and skilled, but will find himself powerless to mobilise himself and the people around him. The same may apply to a shop steward or shop-steward committee. It is quite fashionable to send them out on training courses and they normally become very knowledgeable and skilled, but hesitant and frightened to mobilise those around them to drive the competitive agenda that they have learnt on the course. If they are brave enough to articulate the competitive survival agenda, the chances are they will become alienated from their constituents. The same applies to managers who are sent on these world-class courses, especially human resources managers. They will find it difficult to implement what they have learnt and to gather support of the people who hold power in organisations around the new agenda. The result is that one becomes marginalised and a frustrated hero, as have some human resources managers in the new South Africa.

Normally the diplomatic general managers and managing directors give them limited ceremonial support, such as opening the conference but abandoning them when it comes to confrontation of relevant managers; and during budgeting time they do not give them the required support for the enormous resources required for change processes.

There seems to be enough evidence that the traditional approaches to managing change are training and development. We need to be courageous and examine our own interventions and question their relevance. The issue is what the change agents, particularly human resources practitioners, should do in order to escalate the learning processes in their organisation so as to match the daunting challenges of change, reconstruction and development in Africa.

This is an area where the case for going back to yesterday and known landmarks is valid. What can we learn from traditional African approaches to managing change, education and training? The traditional African education practices focus on the following areas: collective ceremonies and rituals, story tellers, dancing and music as well as facilitation by an outsider, soothsayer and sangoma. The facilitator is always an outsider. In fact, there is a proverb from the African Shona tribe that a thumb, although it is strong, cannot kill aphids on its own. It would require the collective co-operation of the other fingers.

This brings us to a very important African theory in training, which we are going to call The Collective Fingers Theory.

COLLECTIVE FINGERS THEORY

For the thumb to work efficiently it will need the collective co-operation of the other fingers. The managerial lesson to flow from this is that if training and development are going to lead to collective action, they will have to be collective in their approach and practice. For training to move from collective talk to collective action it will need to harness the collective energy and support of the key players in the organisation. It means that one needs to open collective forums, which are inclusive in nature and must, as much as possible, include everyone in the organisation.

**COLLECTIVE DEVELOPMENT &
RECONSTRUCTION**

PHASE 1

Change training must, as much as possible, be residential and off site and it must last 3 - 5 days to allow the creation and development of a learning community. It needs to be led by an outside facilitator who becomes a latter-day soothsayer. The training must focus on a converging survival theme, but must allow space for other gut issues so that people can grapple with their own shadows. It cannot be sequential, rational and factual. The training sessions must be punctuated by ritual and ceremony in order to initiate a bonding process, which is vital for solidarity learning. The ceremonial aspects are as important as the factual aspects.

It is difficult to build a learning process from facts and logical processes. One has to build in the seemingly irrational and emotional ritual aspects such as singing, dancing, playing and humour as well as story telling. It is said a powerful slide must be accompanied by a humorous personal story. The personal disclosure by the facilitator and the ability to tell stories and take a personal risk are critical. The participants want a personal connection and a personal touch. They are looking not just for facts, but personal intimacy, sincerity, simplicity and development. Ideally, the approach is to take top management on a strategic "bosberaad" for 3 - 5 days which must be totally African in both its content and processes. It must incorporate music and an African evening function, possibly the Nkosikazi or women or spouses can join for the evening function. During the evening function there must be fireside story telling by an outside expert on a particular survival topic for not more than an hour.

PHASE 2

The next phase of the change training should be an inclusive 3-day "bosberaad" for all key players, including shop-floor people who wield power and influence. The ritual and ceremonial aspects are also very important, particularly the evening function and inviting an outside story teller to embroider on a particular survival theme.

PHASE 3

The third phase of change training and development should now include the critical mass of the whole company in the form of inclusive strategic forums. The ceremonial aspects are even more important at this level to facilitate bonding. At the third level the composition of participants must be multilevel, cross-functional and multiracial if it is going to lead to collective action.

These three phases prepare the organisation and the individual for the learning challenge and help to clarify the survival issues and build a shared will to survive.

PHASE 4

The next stage has to do with helping the organisation to build the capacity and skill. This requires the organisation to undertake a participative skills audit without suspicion. Individual training and development plans are then drawn up. Most skills training in the traditional society is through mentors and "doing". The traditional approach therefore emphasises practical action and a close, trustful and helpful relationship with the mentors in terms of coaching and interpersonal skills. The focus must be on the importance of ceremonial and ritual aspects of the relationship which facilitates the bonding process.

PHASE 5

The fifth aspect is training the trainees to be learners. How do trainees optimise the learning opportunities that the daily problems, encounters and activities offer? The idea is to teach them to be self-empowered and authors of their own destiny so that they can mobilise the resources and people around them to help them on their learning journey.

The other important area of training in Africa is how to access relevant information by all employees in the organisation. The traditional methods of memos, notice boards and handing out notices with payslips have not been very effective. Africa seems to prefer the personal touch in communication, therefore the ritual of ceremonies, aspects of education and information giving are very important.

We suggest that one of the most important traditions in African nationalistic resistance and culture is mass rallies and that this should be adapted to strategic competitive issues in the environment. The managing directors should address the workers on important strategic issues on a regular basis, at least every quarter. The communication by leaders must not be factual but must make extensive use of symbols, story telling, music and rituals. When an event happens it must be accompanied by pomp, ceremony and ritual. Bring in a choir when the company results are announced or have a braai. This will facilitate the bonding and development of the company spirit. The managing director must not suppress the rhythm of the African spirit, therefore dancing, food and story telling are important elements of a mass rally.

There must be one annual production, quality or world-class festival day to celebrate the achievement of the company. Spouses must be invited and a ceremonial cow must be slaughtered. The daily events must be punctuated by short speeches on at least three strategic themes and the event must be accompanied by music, food and entertainment. The company must strive to distance itself from the formal, rigid and unemotional approach of the West, which is dull and meaningless to those who are unaccustomed to it.

CONCLUSION

The view of the authors in this chapter is that the challenges of Reconstruction and Development in Africa will require new collective approaches to training and development. It will necessitate going back to our African roots and yet still grasping the new approaches from Western and Eastern experiences. We need an integrated and collective approach to development. It would require the awakening of the remarkable survival spirit of the dispossessed, poor individuals in African organisations.

We need the courage to create a new and innovative solution process for South Africa. Ideas from other countries are essential, they will help us to improve our performance in organisations, but the best they can offer in terms of competitive positioning is competitive parity rather than advantage. In order to have competitive advantage in the global marketplace, Africa has to do something different and uniquely African. Fortunately for us the great things in Africa are yet to be done in the competitive game, there are no permanent winners or losers and the place for Africa awaits.

CHAPTER

THE RELEVANCE OF THE AFRICAN VILLAGE IN ORGANISATIONAL DESIGN

We have left the villages far behind
The words can no longer be said,
Can no longer express.

Excerpt from **Poems** by Eva Bezwoda, *Villages*

The debate central to the issue of managing organisational transformation in South Africa is the kind of new society and institutions we are creating. This complicates corporate renewal efforts in South Africa. In the developed economies, the issue was resolved some 30 or 40 years ago. Therefore the focus for them, with regard to managing corporate change, is about how to arrange things better and how to do things more efficiently. These issues remain important for managers in Africa, but their task of managing corporate change is complicated by the debate on the nature of the new society and its institutions, which have to be created. Therefore for us in South Africa the ability to manage and understand normative change is very important if corporate transformation is to be managed efficiently. We have to define the nature of the business institution that we have to create if business is going to thrive in the new South Africa.

One major problem which is causing change initiatives to fail in South Africa is that they are undertaken with the unrealistic assumption that the organisational design in terms of structure, authority and relationships will remain untouched. There is evidence that the form of our businesses in terms of organisational design is being challenged by the current sociopolitical and socioeconomic changes taking place, not only in South Africa but also in the global context. The organisational design that is emerging is something far removed from the known industrial organisation to a much more feudal style that can only be found in its original form in Africa.

It would appear that the traditional African village is striving to reassert itself in the modern South African organisation. The types of issues and characteristics that are being hotly debated are very reminiscent of the African village. These are issues such as the need to create trust, multiple stakeholder accountability, group care, and loyalty. There is also emphasis on participation and inclusive structures and governance. In fact, there is also an awareness by companies regarding the need to create rituals and ceremonies to celebrate their achievements and to mourn their misfortunes. This is a clear testimony that the mechanical, scientific attempt to marginalise primitive human feelings and run organisations purely on rational logic has failed. Indeed there is a clarion call for community creation in organisations which is a call to retain the collective bonds of the traditional African village.

The task of organisational design in the new South Africa is about crafting into the modern South African organisation the community attributes of an African village. We need to create enterprising communities with the freedom to enterprise.

This will occur if the following changes are undertaken in South African companies:

- We need to move from a single shareholder accountability to multiple stakeholder accountability and transparency.

- We need to move from efficient resource utilisation to effective resource optimisation by harnessing the community spirit that lies dormant in our companies.

- We need to move from exclusive governance and performance structures to inclusive governance and performance structures.

- We need to move from professional and managerial prerogatives to demystified participative performance and decision making.

- We need to move from adversarial relationships characterised by a high degree of mistrust, intolerance, polarisation and alienation to unity in diversity, characterised by a high degree of mutual trust, respect, co-operation and racial, political, tribal and cultural tolerance.

- There is a need for movement away from the current mode of hidden agendas to the creation of **negotiated** common stakeholder agendas.

- There is a need to move from the management of people and resources to the mobilisation process of people and resources.

- There is a need to move from lifetime specialisation to a lifetime multiskilling.

- There is a need to move from lifetime job security to lifetime worklife security.

BEST PRACTISES

Most organisations in Africa, because of the competitive global forces, had no choice but to downsize. In most cases this meant the removal of middle management layers as their functions were increasingly reallocated to lower levels in the organisation. In fact, the development and evolution of competitive advantage has lead to this position. Most of the best practices such as "Just in Time" (JIT) and Statistical Process Control (SPC), Total Quality Management (TQM) and Total Productive Maintenance (TPM) have ensured effective empowerment of nonmanagerial levels in the organisation and eradicated management levels in the organisation. This also has changed the organisational design from functional specialists to multiskilled teams just as it is in an ordinary village. There is also an emphasis on constant skill acquisition, just as it is in the village. The specialists in the village are always eager to share information and expertise with those around them through systematic on-the-job coaching.

Our message is that if the emerging form of South African business is going to be enhanced, there will be a need to go back to the African villages and seek in-depth understanding of how a village functions, extracting relevant elements and bringing them back to the corporation. We feel the following aspects of the village are very essential for our companies:

BRINGING THE VILLAGE EXPERIENCE INTO THE COMPANY

- Villages function through a process of grass-roots democracy in the form of open discussion forums on key issues that affect the village. These forums are called "indabas" in Zulu or "dane" in Shona or "khotlas" in Tswana. We feel if South African companies are going to be effective, they need to create open shop-floor forums at the shop-floor level as well as inclusive forums throughout the organisation to discuss competitive and survival issues. The important thing is that these forums must be inclusive and must have an aspect of open agendas. There has to be space to discuss issues which are not part of the agenda.

- A village is characterised by rituals and ceremonies to celebrate achievements and to share misfortunes. Sophisticated companies in South Africa need to create relevant rituals with an African context rather than just extracting Western rituals whose content and form may be alienating to the majority of workers. The hallmark of village rituals is that they are both formal and informal. The sharing of rewards recognises the team involvement through celebrations. The rituals are also part of community sharing and recognition of rewards.

- Although there is tremendous participation and consultation, position, authority and expertise are respected. This brings an element of order and stability into the African tribal village. It is an element which we feel should be incorporated into the modern African organisation. The current wave of empowerment is not going to turn into mob rule.

- The village is based on mutual trust, respect and care. We feel that this is an element that modern South African organisations should enhance and convert into a competitive edge.

- The village also thrives on the bond of collective unity and a common agenda. This is very important for modern South African organisations that have been conceived in a divided society. If South African companies are going to be competitive, they need to emphasise company solidarity not through speeches, but rituals. They also need to negotiate a common agenda with all stakeholders.

- In a traditional African village it is assumed that problems do not have a final solution. Therefore it is always important to discuss issues in order to come up with an acceptable, but not final, solution.

It is important for managers to build ceremonies where problems can be discussed continuously and solutions reached. The element of "talks about talks" is critical for survival of the company.

In a village there is no such thing as permanent job security. What villages have is permanent worklife security based on continuous skill acquisition from others in the community. If this aspect is brought into the company, it would enable people to adjust to the realities of rightsizing.

In a village, people gain recognition and status through contribution. It is high time this aspect is incorporated so that people are paid and given recognition according to contribution and not hierarchical boxes. It is not farfetched because the knowledge professions in organisations have started doing this, such as in academic institutions.

FINAL REFLECTIONS

As we sit and reflect on the future of our mother continent, we feel excited that despite the constraints created by underdevelopment and poverty, the future for us looks very rosy. We like what we are seeing.

The question that people may ask is about the problems of post colonial Africa. We do not see that negatively. There can be no transformation without decay otherwise there will be no space to reach for the new germination. The decay in post colonial Africa is a necessary condition for the transformation of Africa. The question is what is the way forward for Africa and its organisations.

Our view is that the creative force of history is not ideology or religion or politics. It is the way people organise work and create value. It was the factory system that brought men out of cottage industry and feudal conditions. It was mass production that brought about the current mass consumption civilisation and its throwaway technology. America's fame was as a result of its ability to master mass production techniques. It is world-class manufacturing techniques that have brought the current information revolution. Japan's ascent into global significance was as a result of its ability to master world-class manufacturing techniques.

It is our rallying call that Africa must master the world-class production techniques and then reach out for mass customisation before any other country in the world. African soothsayers and intellectuals must shift their attention from the politics of resistance to the politics of production, from the fascination with European literature to the fascination for their own roots, which are steeped in the myths and rituals of Africa. It is only then that we will have the confidence to create economic growth.

SELECTED BIBLIOGRAPHY

Arien, A. 1993. *The Four-Fold Way: Walking the Paths of The Warrior, Teacher, Healer and Visionary.* San Francisco: Harper Collins.

Bezwoda, E. 1994. *Poems.* Johannesburg: Workbench.

Buker, D W. 1993. *Top Management's Guide to World Class Manufacturing.* Kansas City: Lowell Press.

Barker, J A. 1992. *Paradigms: The Business of Discovering The Future.* New York: Harper Business.

Covey, S R. 1989. *The Seven Habits of Highly Effective People.* London: Simon & Schuster.

Handy, C. 1985. *Gods of Management. The Changing Work of Organisations.* London: Pan Books.

Lapping, B. 1986. *Apartheid, A History.* London: Paladin Grafton Books.

Lessem, R. 1989. *Global Management Principles.* London: Prentice Hall.

Lessem, R *et al.* 1993. *African Management: Philosophies, Concepts and Applications.* Randburg: Knowledge Resources.

Mahola, M. 1994. *Strange Things.* Plumstead: Snailpress.

Mattera, D. 1994. *Azanian Love Songs.* Johannesburg: Justified Press.

Omotoso, K. 1994. *Season of Migration to the South: Africa's Crisis Reconsidered.* Cape Town: Tafelberg.

Owen, H. 1987. *Spirit, Transformation and Development in Organisations.* Potomac: Abbott Publishing.

Senge, P. 1990. *The Fifth Discipline: The Art and Practice of the Learning Organization.* London: Double Day Currency.

Soyinka, W. 1975. *Poems of Black Africa.* Portsmouth: Heineman.

Veit-Wild, F. 1992. *Dambudzu Marechera. A Sourcebook on his Life and Work.* London: Hans Zell.

OTHER PRODUCTS FROM

Knowledge Resources provides individuals and companies with the materials necessary to achieve excellence in leadership, marketing, human resources management, strategic management, quality, productivity and general management.

Contact us today for further information on our products and services on:

Tel: International +27 +11 + 880-8540
Fax: International +27 +11 + 880-8700
E-mail: knowres@aztec.co.za
Postal Address: P O Box 3954
                  RANDBURG
                  2125
                  SOUTH AFRICA

****

UBUNTU
The Spirit of African Transformation Management
Lovemore Mbigi with Jenny Maree

Africa needs to draw on its triple cultural heritage from Africa, the East and the West. The starting point should be our own roots if we are to meet the challenges of development and reconstruction.

AFRICAN MANAGEMENT
Philosophies, Concepts & Applications
Peter Christie, Ronnie Lessem, Lovemore Mbigi (eds.)

The management of organisations in Africa has been largely neglected by the mainstream literature. This is the first book to comprehensively deal with the topic of African management and is highly applicable to the changing South African situation.

AFFIRMATIVE ACTION
A "how to" guide for managers
Thea Wingrove

Here is a book which has been endorsed by the Black community across the broad spectrum which gives practical examples of the effective implementation of a custom-made affirmative action model for every organisational environment.

PEOPLE REALLY MATTER
South African Companies Learn Tough Lessons
Mike Alfred & Meave Potter

Are people really important? This book features a series of Manpower Briefs written over the past few years. It offers a wide-ranging picture of the human issues faced by South African businesses and provides some significant answers!